BILLY BARRETT

Billy is a director, writer and co-Artistic Director of Breach. Previous work for the company includes *It's True, It's True, It's True*, a courtroom drama re-staging a seventeenth-century rape trial which was broadcast on BBC4, and *The Beanfield*, a multimedia show about police violence and civil liberties in 1980's Britain. With Breach, he is currently researching and developing a documentary theatre piece about the undercover policing scandal, as well as a new play about the true story behind Ibsen's *A Doll's House*. Billy has worked with writers on new plays as both a director and dramaturg, and led workshops in documentary and devised theatre for organisations including the National Theatre, Old Vic Theatre and the Roundhouse. As a visiting director, he has directed devised theatre productions as well as musicals at drama schools including RADA and Guildhall.

ELLICE STEVENS

Ellice is a writer, performer and co-Artistic Director of Breach. Her co-writing for Breach has been awarded two Scotsman Fringe First Awards (*Tank* and *It's True, It's True, It's True*), and she was part of the ensemble that was awarded *The Stage* Edinburgh Award for Acting (*It's True, It's True, It's True*). She has performed in all but one of Breach's stage productions. She has worked with companies such as Barrel Organ and The Handlebards. Most recently she has performed in Breach's short film *Gaia* which premiered at BFI Flare, the short film *Hearts & Aubergines* directed by Daniel Lundh, and has directed a two-hander of *Macbeth* for The Handlebards.

FREW

Frew has a Master's degree in Conducting and Composition from the University of Hull. He is currently under commission from the Almeida Theatre to compose a new musical. Composition credits include *Chariots of Fire*, *Steel* (Sheffield Theatres); *The Canary and the Crow*, *Us Against Whatever*, *One Life Stand*, *I Hate Alone*, *Mercury Fur*, *Weekend Rockstars: An Album Play* (with Hull Truck), *Modern Life Is Rubbish: A Musical Manifesto*, *Saturday Night, Sunday Morning* (Middle Child Theatre); *Joan of Leeds* (New Diorama/Breach Theatre); *The Hundred and One Dalmatians*, *Folk* (Birmingham Rep); *All We Ever Wanted Was Everything* (Bush Theatre/Edinburgh Festival/Middle Child); *Get Carter* (Northern Stage/UK tour); *Twelfth Night* (Orange Tree); *Sketching* (Wilton's Music Hall); *Mixtape* (Royal Exchange); *Rapunzel*, *Sleeping Beauty*, *Cinderella*, *A Taste of Honey* (Hull Truck); and *The Thing About Psychopaths* (Red Ladder Theatre/National Tour).

Billy Barrett and Ellice Stevens

AFTER THE ACT

Music by Frew

NICK HERN BOOKS
London
www.nickhernbooks.co.uk

A Nick Hern Book

After the Act first published in Great Britain as a paperback original in 2024 by Nick Hern Books Limited, The Glasshouse, 49a Goldhawk Road, London W12 8QP, in association with Breach Theatre

After the Act copyright © 2024 Billy Barrett and Ellice Stevens

Billy Barrett and Ellice Stevens have asserted their right to be identified as the authors of this work

Cover design by Rebecca Pitt

Designed and typeset by Nick Hern Books, London
Printed in Great Britain by Mimeo Ltd, Huntingdon, Cambridgeshire PE29 6XX

A CIP catalogue record for this book is available from the British Library

ISBN 978 1 83904 398 7

CAUTION All rights whatsoever in this play are strictly reserved. Requests to reproduce the text in whole or in part should be addressed to the publisher.

Amateur Performing Rights Applications for performance, including readings and excerpts, by amateurs in the English language should be addressed to the Performing Rights Manager, Nick Hern Books, The Glasshouse, 49a Goldhawk Road, London W12 8QP, *tel* +44 (0)20 8749 4953, *email* rights@nickhernbooks.co.uk, except as follows:

Australia: ORiGiN Theatrical, *tel* +61 (2) 8514 5201, *email* enquiries@originmusic.com.au, *web* www.origintheatrical.com.au

New Zealand: Play Bureau, 20 Rua Street, Mangapapa, Gisborne 4010, *tel* +64 21 258 3998, *email* info@playbureau.com

USA and Canada: Independent Talent, see details below.

Professional Performing Rights Application for performance by professionals in any medium and in any language throughout the world should be addressed to Independent Talent Group Ltd, 40 Whitfield Street, London W1T 2RH, *tel* +44 (020) 7636 6565

No performance of any kind may be given unless a licence has been obtained. Applications should be made before rehearsals begin. Publication of this play does not necessarily indicate its availability for amateur performance.

www.nickhernbooks.co.uk/environmental-policy

Acknowledgements

After the Act is a show about many different voices coming together, and so it's perhaps appropriate that creating it was a monumentally collective effort. Beyond our credited collaborators, we're grateful to the following people for helping us bring this absurdly ambitious piece to the stage:

On the research front, we're indebted to the author Paul Baker and his fantastically gripping book *Outrageous! The Story of Section 28 and Britain's Battle for LGBT Education*. This wide-reaching and meticulously cited account helped us connect the dots of the timeline and scope of Section 28, and its publication halfway through the show's development filled a gap in the literature that we, and readers in general, were desperately missing. We recommend it to anyone wanting to further their understanding of the subject. Davina Cooper's *Sexing the City: Lesbian and Gay Politics Within the Activist State*, which includes recollections and analysis of her time at Haringey Council in the 1980s, was also instrumental for us in conceiving the show's 'Ordinary Mums and Dads' sequence.

Our access to a vast trove of original sources would not have been possible without the efforts of archivists over the years to compile and preserve records of British queer activism and media coverage. The Lesbian and Gay Newsmedia Archive at the Bishopsgate Institute provided us with a fascinating window into the (generally grim) public attitudes towards gay people in the 1980s, as well as a clear picture of the ways in which the right-wing press stoked the hysteria that led to Section 28. Veronica McKenzie's Vanguard Collection at the Haringey Archive, meanwhile, gave us a vivid and inspiring overview of the activities of Haringey-based community activists through oral histories, council documents and campaign materials. Thank you to Julie Melrose at the Haringey Archives for your help, and for your generosity in granting image rights for the video design in our production. Both of these collections also house some of the few precious copies of *Jenny Lives with Eric and Martin,* which would otherwise have set us back over a hundred pounds on eBay.

Another archivist we would like to thank is perhaps better known for his work in other fields – Sir Ian McKellen, who kindly spoke with us and allowed us to spend the day trawling through his basement collection of correspondence and photographs relating to Section 28, the Arts Lobby and Stonewall. The role played by well-known arts professionals including Sir Ian in organising against Section 28 didn't make it into our final show (they would no doubt tell it better than we ever could), but did help us find our title – a tribute to the 1988 gala performance *Before the Act.* This fundraising evening of works by gay and lesbian writers to support the fight against the Clause was put on by Sir Ian and Michael Cashman among others, and is recalled in detail in Bev Ayres' excellent podcast of the same name. We're proud to continue the tradition, in our own small way, of theatre fighting against the impact of Section 28.

As ever, we would like to thank David Byrne, Sophie Wallis and the team at New Diorama for their support and trust in us as a company – and for making us feel like anything was possible. David, you told us this was the riskiest show you'd ever programmed and that you wouldn't have accepted this pitch from anyone else. Thank you for waiting until the show was open to tell us that, and for your late-night show notes and encouragement during a truly wild week of previews. In the same vein, we're grateful to Rachel Twigg and the National Theatre Studio for allowing us the time and space to figure out whether this idea might work, and for putting up with a week of us harmonising homophobic obscenities.

Over the course of the show's development, we've been lucky enough to work with a brilliant collection of queer performers, singers and musicians, who have lent us their voices and fed in their ideas and experiences. The final show is the product of everyone who took part in those initial workshops: Rachel Barnes,

Dior Clarke, Emer Dineen, Sarah Farrell, Len Blanco, Marina Papadopoulos, Alex Roberts, Lucy Stepan and Yasser Zadeh. We also had the great privilege of working with Tika Mu'tamir, Ellian Showering and EM Williams in the initial production – thank you so much for coming on that journey with us and for all that you brought to the show.

Finally, a heartfelt thanks to all of our interviewees who so generously trusted us with their stories, and who in speaking with us helped to fill the void of over three decades of silence. Our conversations spanned the length and breadth of the UK and several different generations, and their common themes and echoed experiences helped us feel less alone – particularly in the isolated, post-Covid weeks when we first began this project. This show is for you, and for everyone else who wasn't able to learn about who they were during those dark years of Section 28.

Billy Barrett and Ellice Stevens

Director's Note

When you ask children of the late '80s and early '90s about their memories of Section 28, or being taught anything about gay people at school, they most likely won't have much to say – the very essence of the Act was censorship and absence. But that was one of the questions Ellice and I put to ex-students, teachers, activists and historians at the outset of this project, as we tried to piece together the story of the legislation to mark the twenty-year anniversary of its repeal.

Because for us, researching *After the Act* was as much an attempt to fill in the gaps of our own knowledge as those of our audience. As '90's kids, we weren't around for the febrile ideological clashes or headline-grabbing protests that preceded Section 28. We grew up under its shadow – with coy half-answers from teachers and casual homophobia a part of daily life at school. I'm pretty sure I only really found out that that silence and ambiguity had been government-mandated long after I'd actually left. This was despite growing up in Haringey – a London borough, I'd later learn, that just a few years earlier had been one of the most infamous hotspots of the Section 28 culture wars.

As I heard more about it occasionally over the years, the idea for a show about Section 28 quietly began to form in the back of my mind. The Haringey connection fascinated me – as did the fact that I have no memories of the Clause being repealed halfway through my time at school, or of any particularly inclusive messaging afterwards. At a certain point, I realised that I knew almost nothing about this thing that had such a fundamental impact on my growing up and making sense of my place in the world – and nor, it seemed, did many other people my age. It was as if the Clause had successfully prohibited knowledge even of its own existence.

But by the time I pitched the idea to Ellice and our composer Frew, in 2021, Section 28 was making its way back into the national conversation – less because of its impending anniversary than because many queer people were arguing that it was being resuscitated in a new form via the vicious backlash against trans rights. It only takes a cursory look through the coverage of Section 28 at the time to see the connections between fear-mongering around 'positive images' of gays and lesbians in schools, and the demonisation of trans-inclusive education and young people's access to gender-affirming services today. Ellice and I had by then spent six or seven years honing our approaches to verbatim and documentary theatre, and had developed not only a rapacious appetite for an archive but a conviction that the struggles of our present are often seen most clearly from the distance of the past. There are stories that wait to be told – and this one, we decided, was ready to be heard.

So on our first day of research, we walked into Gay's The Word bookshop on Marchmont Street – the logical starting point of any queer history project – ready to learn all about Section 28. There wasn't a single book about it. Similarly, no one we spoke to around that time could recommend a documentary, or even a play or novel that gave a full account of how the legislation was enacted and the impact it had. Of course, it was likely to feature as *context*, or a subplot, to any '80's queer story – everyone now remembers the books being taken off school library shelves in *It's a Sin*. But despite its enormity, the Clause never seemed to be the main event. We suddenly found ourselves hit by the daunting scale of the task ahead – as well as a ridiculous burden of responsibility. Were we going to have to scrap this whole musical idea and instead create a vast oral history project, just so this stuff was actually written down somewhere?

Thankfully, we were far from the only ones to have the idea to mark the anniversary, and subsequently a whole wave of books, films and performance projects specifically about Section 28 and its legacy has begun to emerge with various different angles on the subject, of which we're proud to be a part. This relieved us of the impossible remit of a fully comprehensive account, allowing us to hone in on the events and personal testimonies that spoke most vividly to us.

Perhaps the main reason that so few people (or seemingly, none) have set out to dramatise the story of Section 28 itself is that no single character or even small group of characters can tell it from start to finish. This is a story involving many different campaign groups and politicians across the country, over a number of years, fighting over an arcane piece of legislation that ended up affecting literally everyone that went to a state school. We realised very quickly that finding the through-line and dramatic structure was going to be a challenge. A fictional protagonist – one possible solution – felt unfaithful in some way to the documentary and verbatim nature of the endeavour. Instead, we realised, the show had to wholeheartedly embrace the notion of one character passing the baton to the next – in a decades-long relay, running through classrooms, news studios, the Houses of Parliament, all the way up to the present day.

Structurally, then, the show is chronological – with the exception of the first scene, which functions as a sort of cold open, and the last, which acts as a final flashback. Thatcher's power ballad 'Cheated' is also dropped in out of sequence at the top of Act Two, as a drag-inspired fever dream that sets up the bleaker scenes that follow. The full text is probably about seventy-five per cent verbatim; the majority of its words are drawn from our own interviews, as well as Hansard (the record of all parliamentary debates) and other archival materials. These were, of course, then cut up, edited and reordered for the score as well as for narrative. Substantial dialogue, for example from the parents in 'Ordinary Mums and Dads', is adapted from and fairly close to original sources including vox pops from the time.

The show is a musical; that was essential to its conception. Partly, the music is intended as a theatrical unifier, to chorally bring together disparate narrative strands and fragmented scenes. It is also a little strategic – a Trojan horse of a glittering, camp spectacle housing a documentary theatre piece that might have otherwise sounded just too depressing or earnest. But perhaps most importantly, the music has always been about

DIRECTOR'S NOTE

making a lot of noise – of filling the silence, however trite that might sound, and of literally vocalising something of the exuberance of the queer community from the 1980s to today.

In fact, the show very much grew out of an existing collaboration with our composer, Frew, and a curiosity to discover together what our take on a verbatim musical might be. The key reference for us all at that point was, of course, *London Road* – Alecky Blythe and Adam Cork's virtuosic verbatim musical about local residents' reactions to the serial murders in Ipswich. That piece proved that such a thing was even possible, and pioneered a technique of scoring and emphasising the natural patter and intonation of their interviewees' speech. We ended up taking quite a different approach – partly from the desire to carve out our own style and follow Frew's musical instincts, and partly because we worked from a combination of recorded and transcribed or otherwise written text.

We also leant heavily into musical references from the era, which Frew is a master at, and had a lot of fun ironically smashing together form and content. Frew's idea for a Billy Bragg-style protest anthem for the fiercely conservative 'Ordinary Mums and Dads', for example, makes it unexpectedly moving – whilst 'Roll the Dice', which cuts together horrendous tabloid bile about the dangers of AIDS and the need to curb the 'promotion' of homosexuality, has poignant and confronting undertones of Bronski Beat's 'Smalltown Boy'.

After the Act has been on quite some journey already, from the three of us sitting around a keyboard in a shed behind New Diorama to the full touring production which we're right now preparing to take on the road for audiences across the country. While this show contains none of our personal experiences explicitly, it resonates with each of us on a deeply personal level, and has taken an almighty collaborative effort to create. We're delighted that it will now have yet another life on these pages for readers to experience – as well as in the hands of anyone who might choose to carry the baton forward in their own production.

Billy Barrett, October 2024

After the Act was first performed at New Diorama Theatre, London, on 28 February 2023 and the Traverse Theatre, Edinburgh, on 3 August 2023. The cast was as follows:

Tika Mu'tamir (she/her)
Ellice Stevens (she/her)
EM Williams (they/them)
Zachary Willis (he/him)

Musical Director and Performer	Frew (he/they)
Musician	Ellian Showering (they/them)
Director	Billy Barrett (he/him)
Writers	Billy Barrett (he/him) and Ellice Stevens (she/her)
Composer, Orchestrator and Co-Music Production	Frew (he/they)
Choreographer	Sung-Im Her (she/her)
Set and Costume Designer	Lizzy Leech (she/her)
Creative Sound Designer and Co-Music Production	Owen Crouch (he/him)
Video Designer	Zakk Hein (he/him)
Associate Video Designer	Hayley Egan (she/her)
Lighting Designer	Jodie Underwood (she/they)
Music Associate	Rachel Barnes (she/her)
Sound System Designer	Ed Clarke (he/him)
Executive Producer	Sally Cowling (she/her)
General Manager	Emily Tate (she/her)
Production Manager/ Technical Stage Manager	Adam Jefferys (he/him)
Lighting Operator	Becky Thornton (she/her)

FOR THE TRAVERSE PERFORMANCES

Executive Producer for New Diorama	Sophie Wallis
Production Manager/ Technical Stage Manager	Paul Milford (he/him)
Lighting Operator	Paddy Hepplewhite (he/him)
Associate Choreographer	Anouk Jouanne (she/her)

After the Act was revived at Liverpool Playhouse on 24 October 2024, before touring the UK. The cast was as follows:

Ericka Posadas (she/they)
Nkara Stephenson (he/they)
Ellice Stevens (she/her)
Zachary Willis (he/him)

Musical Director and Performer Frew (he/they)

Director	Billy Barrett (he/him)
Writers	Billy Barrett (he/him) and Ellice Stevens (she/her)
Composer, Orchestrator and Co-Music Production	Frew (he/they)
Choreographer	Sung-Im Her (she/her)
Set and Costume Designer	Bethany Wells (she/her)
Creative Sound Designer and Co-Music Production	Owen Crouch (he/him)
Video Designer	Zakk Hein (he/him)
Lighting Designer	Jodie Underwood (she/they)
Music Supervisor	Martin Lowe (he/him)
Sound System Designer	Ed Clarke (he/him)
Casting Director	Nick Hockaday (he/him)
Executive Producer	Sally Cowling (she/her)
General Manager	Katie Sherrard (she/her)
Production Manager	Paul Milford (he/him)
Technical Stage Manager	Eliott Sheppard (he/him)
Sound No.1	Matt Coulson (he/him)
Company Stage Manager	Esther Malkinson (she/her)

After the Act was commissioned by New Diorama Theatre and supported by the National Theatre Studio. It premiered at New Diorama Theatre in March 2023. Its production at the Traverse Theatre was co-produced with New Diorama in Association with the Traverse Theatre. Its tour was co-produced by Brighton Dome, HOME, New Diorama and Warwick Arts Centre. Its London production and tour were both supported by Arts Council England.

Touring Production, 2024

Previews: The Albany, Deptford, 17–18 October

Liverpool Playhouse, 24–26 October
New Wolsey Theatre, Ipswich, 29–30 October
Warwick Arts Centre, 1–3 November
Connaught Theatre, Worthing, 6 November
Brighton Corn Exchange, 8–9 November
HOME Manchester, 12–16 November
Minerva Theatre, Chichester Festival Theatre, 27–30 November

~~BREACH~~

Breach is a multi-award-winning devised theatre company founded by Dorothy Allen-Pickard, Billy Barrett and Ellice Stevens. The company works in collaboration with Executive Producer Sally Cowling.

We uncover stories that captivate us – from an experiment into teaching dolphins English, to a rape trial in Renaissance Rome, to the impact of homophobic legislation in the 1980s – using them to provoke alternative perspectives and to illuminate the times in which we live.

There's a rigour to our research and a playfulness to our work: combining a forensic documentary approach with bold and inventive devising. We are always in search of the 'truth' about big issues, without claiming any sort of objectivity ourselves. Our shows are full of subversive humour and unafraid to be political.

Our productions tour nationally and internationally, and have previously been published by Oberon Books. *After the Act* is our first play published by Nick Hern Books.

www.breachtheatre.com

Characters

(*in order of appearance*)

SARAH, *lesbian activist*
CHARLOTTE, *lesbian activist*
SUE LAWLEY, *BBC News presenter*
NICHOLAS WITCHELL, *BBC News presenter*
MARK, *gay ex-student*
CATHERINE, *PE teacher*
MAYA, *spokesperson for the Haringey Council Lesbian and Gay Subcommittee. British Asian*
JENNY, *a character in* Jenny Lives with Eric and Martin
MARTIN, *a character in* Jenny Lives with Eric and Martin
ERIC, *a character in* Jenny Lives with Eric and Martin
PETER, *leader of the Parents' Rights Group*
DAME JILL KNIGHT, *Conservative MP for Edgbaston*
PETER PIKE, *Labour MP for Burnley*
STUART HOLLAND, *Labour MP for Vauxhall*
DANIEL, *gay ex-student*
LB, *ex-student, non-binary*
REVEREND ROBERT SIMPSON, *a vicar*
SIMON HUGHES, *Liberal Democrat MP for Bermondsey and Old Southwark*
ELAINE KELLET-BOWMAN, *Conservative MP for Lancaster*
CHRIS SMITH, *Labour MP for Islington South and Finsbury*
LORD MASON OF BARNSLEY, *Labour*
MARGARET THATCHER, *Prime Minister*
FELIX, *gay ex-student*
IAN, *gay ex-student*
STIFYN PARRI, *actor*
SUE JOHNSTON, *actress*
GRAHAM STRINGER, *Leader of Manchester City Council*

Notes on Characters and Casting

Breach's original production of *After the Act* is performed by a cast of four, playing a large ensemble of characters. It could certainly be performed by a larger cast if desired. Ethnicity or gender identity are specified where they are essential attributes for the character, but otherwise the show is intended to be performed by a diverse cast who are representative of the breadth of British queer experience.

The ensemble all play the parts of unnamed journalists, politicians, parents, schoolchildren and teachers.

In the original production, the Studio Director of *The Six O'Clock News*, the Speaker in the House of Commons and the Lord Speaker are all voiced from offstage by the show's Musical Director.

Notes on Staging

The show is a musical. Brief descriptions of each song's musical style are also given in this script.

Stage directions are intended to give an indication of Breach's original staging, including video, set and costume design.

Breach's touring production is set within a school. Its combination of PE gym bars and platforms, wooden benches, a blackboard and library shelves create a flexible space that is rearranged throughout the show to represent various other public buildings such as the House of Commons, a town hall, etc. It sits beneath visible, fluorescent industrial light fittings which flicker intermittently throughout.

Chronology

Many of the speakers in *After the Act* address the audience directly in the present, but the events described and dramatised are broadly chronological, with a few exceptions. In the original production, rough or specific dates are provided sporadically in the video design. These are as follows:

Act One – Before the Act
Scene One, BBC Studio Invasion: 23rd May, 1988
Scene Two, Gays Were Funny Things: 1984
Scene Three, Positive Images: 1986
Scene Four, Jenny Lives with Eric and Martin: 1986
Scene Five, Ordinary Mums and Dads: 1987
Scene Six, The Act – Committee Stage: 8th May, 1987
Scene Seven, Don't Die of Ignorance: 1980s
Scene Eight, Roll the Dice: 1980s
Scene Nine, The Act – Commons Debate: 1987
Scene Ten, Tennessee Williams: 1988
Scene Eleven, The Act – Lords Debate: 2nd February, 1988

Act Two – After the Act
Scene One, Cheated: 9th October, 1987
Scene Two, A Double Life: 1990s
Scene Three, Book Closed: 1990s
Scene Four, Slightly Odd Behaviour: 1990s
Scene Five, The Silence is Deafening: 1990s
Scene Six, The Legacy: 2021
Scene Seven, The Manchester March: 20th February, 1988

Notes on the Text

After the Act combines spoken and sung dialogue, sometimes within the same sentence.

Text in **bold** in this playtext indicates that the word or phrase is sung. Lyrics are centred rather than left-aligned. Where the text is centre-aligned but not bold, these lines are delivered over music but not sung.

This text went to press before the end of rehearsals and so may differ slightly from the play as performed.

ACT ONE – BEFORE THE ACT

Prologue

Projected on the back wall:

Local Government Act, 1988

Section 28

A local authority shall not—

(a)

intentionally promote homosexuality or publish material with the intention of promoting homosexuality;

(b)

promote the teaching in any maintained school of the acceptability of homosexuality as a pretended family relationship.

The cast enter the classroom, and the lights flicker on. They hold piles of books, boxes of props, objects from the archive they will use to tell their story. As they place these around the stage, their voices come together in a wordless, choral song. They sit around the classroom on benches and gym platforms.

OVERLAPPING VOICES (*pre-recorded*). This is a show about one piece of legislation, told in the words of the people who lived it. Words from activists, students and teachers. From tabloid columns and political speeches. This is a show about silence – a silence that is very, very loud. Twenty years after the Act.

Scene One: BBC Studio Invasion

SARAH *and* CHARLOTTE *step forward.*

SARAH. I think when you are younger as well, there's an element where you are more fearless than like when you are older, you know. I was in my thirties, early thirties.

CHARLOTTE. We just all came together spontaneously, you know, and just, yeah. We were good at it. We were good at nonviolent direct action. We were good at being imaginative as well.

SARAH. And nobody organised us, nobody told us what to do. Different groups came together. You know, it was an amorphous group of people. That was its strength. I think people just couldn't deal with that. Like, 'Who are you?'

CHARLOTTE. 'You've got no leader!'

SARAH. So I dunno who originally came up with the idea, but, um, I knew someone who was working at the BBC. She gave me some tips on, er, I think names of people to say when they got to the gate, 'we've got a meeting with so and so' – didn't we turn up in a black cab to look more authentic? And as if we had money?

CHARLOTTE. We did. We met, um, just on that green by – what's it called? What's that television studio called that's now flats?

SARAH. I know what you mean – on the big triangular green, wasn't it?

CHARLOTTE. Yeah. Anyway, it doesn't matter. We met there with some handcuffs that had been recently purchased and we hailed the cab and went about two seconds up the road. We got stopped by this poor old security guard and he's like,

SARAH (*in a West Country accent*). 'You're not on my list.'

CHARLOTTE. Don't do the voice.

SARAH. Sorry – (*In her own voice*.) 'You're not on my list.'

Archive footage of the BBC television studio and control rooms is projected.

CHARLOTTE. Um, and he said, 'Okay, go straight to reception.' And, of course, we didn't. We ran up the back stairs.

SARAH. There were a lot of stairs to run up!

They run and climb on top of a school bench, and frantically dress in 'Stop the Clause' T-shirts.

CHARLOTTE. We went in the toilets. We put on our 'Stop the Clause' T-shirts.

SARAH. Brilliant.

CHARLOTTE. And we tried to time it. There's an outer door. It just has a number on it. It doesn't say anything at all. We found the correct number and then we were in a tiny bit of corridor. To one side was the, you know, the control room where they've got all the monitors and that, and then above the door are the, the green and red lights. So we waited in that corridor. And the adrenaline was really pumping.

SARAH. I was out of breath. Might have been the stairs, though.

CHARLOTTE. And then when the light went green, we rushed straight in!

They run into the news studio, where SUE LAWLEY *and* NICHOLAS WITCHELL *are sat on a bench, and jump up behind them, trying to be seen on camera.* SUE LAWLEY *and* NICHOLAS WITCHELL *frantically try to remove them before the live broadcast begins.*

SARAH. Stop Section 28!

CHARLOTTE. We're protesting about rights for lesbian and gay people!

The studio DIRECTOR*'s voice comes from offstage.*

DIRECTOR. Oh fucking hell, we've got nutters in the studio.

CHARLOTTE. This is Clause 28, it affects the rights of twelve per cent of Great Britain and you don't care!

SARAH. Stop the homophobic Clause!

SUE LAWLEY. Get out!

DIRECTOR. Run titles!

The Six O'Clock News *titles play. During this:*

SUE LAWLEY. Get security quickly! Get security, quickly!

DIRECTOR. Get her out! Give her one!

NICHOLAS WITCHELL. I'm trying to give her one, but she won't sit still!

DIRECTOR. Run Camera A. Run B.

SARAH. Lock onto the desk!

CHARLOTTE *handcuffs herself to the newsdesk.*

DIRECTOR. Cue Sue. On air!

SUE LAWLEY. Oh god!

CHARLOTTE *is handcuffed to* SUE LAWLEY*'s bench, whilst* SARAH *is straddled and restrained by* NICHOLAS WITCHELL. *The two activists' mouths are gagged by the presenters' hands. The title card for* The Six O'Clock News *is projected.*

ANNOUNCER (*pre-recorded*). *The Six O'Clock News* from the BBC with Sue Lawley and Nicholas Witchell.

SUE LAWLEY *looks straight down the 'camera' and perseveres with presenting the headlines, despite the continuing physical struggle with the two silenced activists.*

SUE LAWLEY. Good evening. The headlines at six o'clock.

In the House of Lords a vote is taking place now on a **challenge to the poll tax**.

Tory rebels have said that the tax is **unfair and unpopular**. Lord Whitehorse told them that they should not be **confronting the elected chamber**.

We'll be going over to the House of **Lords for the result**. There are to be **changes in the ways nurses work and are trained** –

Changes to stop them leaving the profession. Another prosecution involving undercover police and alleged football hooligans has collapsed. **No evidence was offered.**

Also tonight –

The activists free themselves and sing a defiant chant over the top of SUE LAWLEY*'s presenting.*

SARAH *and* CHARLOTTE.
**Stop Section 28
Stop Section 28
Stop Section 28
Stop Section 28
Stop Section 28
Stop the Clause!**

SUE LAWLEY.
Glasnost gives us a glimpse of inside of the Soviet Army. And with one week to go before the fourth summit, we have reports from Washington and Moscow on the preparations Mr Reagan and Mr Gorbechev are making for their meeting. And repairing the roads – why the closed roads signal a lot more chaos this summer.

SARAH *and* CHARLOTTE.
**Stop Section 28
Stop Section 28
Stop Section 28
Stop the Clause!**

CHARLOTTE *knocks* SUE LAWLEY*'s papers out of her hands and they cascade through the air.* SUE LAWLEY *and* NICHOLAS WITCHELL *freeze as if in a photograph, reacting to the chaos.* SARAH *and* CHARLOTTE *step out of the scene and turn to address the audience once again.*

SARAH. There was a huge amount of media coverage. I mean, I have a whole archive of clippings of the time. But none of it said anything serious about Clause 28.

CHARLOTTE. No.

SARAH. It all went for the sort of titillating angle of –

The actors playing SARAH, CHARLOTTE and NICHOLAS WITCHELL take on the role of tabloid JOURNALISTS gleefully reporting on the events to the audience. Their newspaper headlines are projected.

JOURNALISTS.
**A gaggle of screeching, lesbian harridans.
A gang of screaming lesbians.
Dotty dykes who do their cause
nothing but harm.**

**Four spikey-haired women in jeans and boots,
Hirsute harpies, Loony lezzies,
Tricked their way into
the BBC.**

They lunged at newscaster –

SUE LAWLEY.
Sue Lawley.

JOURNALISTS.
**As she read *The Six O'Clock News*.
Miss Lawley was coolness itself.**

JOURNALIST. They were just inches from sitting on camera when Nicholas Witchell pounced on them. Sat on a protester's chest.

JOURNALISTS.
**He used one hand to keep her on the floor
and clamped the other over her mouth.
Sue remarked regally:**

SUE LAWLEY. And I do apologise if you're hearing quite a lot of noise in the studio at the moment. I'm afraid we have rather been invaded by some people who we hope to be removing fairly shortly.

JOURNALISTS.
**While Sue was merely *presenting* the news
they were trying to *make* the news**

SCENE ONE: BBC STUDIO INVASION

**And influence the nation's thinking
over the reasoned and reasonable Bill
to prevent homosexual propaganda in the classroom.**

JOURNALIST. Women everywhere can today choose between two contrasting models of femininity: Miss Lawley or –

JOURNALISTS.
**A gaggle of screeching, lesbian, harridans.
A gang of screaming lesbians.
Dotty dykes who do their cause nothing but harm.**

**Four spikey-haired women in jeans and boots,
Hirsute harpies, Loony lezzies,
Penetrating Auntie Beeb!**

The JOURNALISTS *join* SUE LAWLEY *in the studio, who is a little shaken up, and relieved that the ordeal is now over. One comfortingly hands her a cup of tea. They all eagerly copy down her responses to their questions in notepads.*

JOURNALIST. When did you first notice the kerfuffle, Sue?

SUE LAWLEY. Well, the studio doors are usually being banged open about that time with people with late news, but what you don't expect is two rather large ladies rushing towards you with handcuffs. You start to worry.

JOURNALIST. But you were so brave.

SUE LAWLEY. Oh, no – it was Nick who performed the heroics. Mine was the boring response, to just carry on with the news.

JOURNALIST. So calm.

JOURNALIST. So elegant.

JOURNALIST. Plucky Sue!

SUE LAWLEY. Well to be honest –

**My knees were shaking,
My heart was pounding.
I couldn't just ignore what was happening.
The whole nation could hear that something was going on –**

                        ALL.
The whole nation could hear that something was going on!

                      SUE LAWLEY.
**My knees were shaking,
My heart was pounding.
I couldn't just ignore what was happening.
The whole nation could hear that something was going on!**

                      JOURNALISTS.
**A gaggle of screeching, lesbian, harridans,
A gang of screaming lesbians.
Dotty dykes who do their cause nothing but harm.
Four spikey haired women in jeans and boots,
Hirsute harpies, Loony lezzies,
Penetrating Auntie, something was going on.**

                        ALL.
The whole nation could hear that something was going on!

Scene Two: Gays Were Funny Things

The classroom.

MARK *and other* SCHOOLBOYS *put on their school ties.*

MARK. So its like, I was er, state, Catholic, comprehensive – I had fucking, the works to go against – you know religion, state school so it was underfunded, falling to pieces, broken windows everywhere, heating quite often didn't work, it was like, single sex, so it was just boys.

The BOYS *play-fight and muck around as they set up the room – rows of seating facing a blackboard.*

But like, living in Manchester on any street, anywhere in that city, the people on that street would not, not know a gay person. It's just, it just, it was just unimaginable. And, and to that extent, like my mum didn't think her hairdresser was gay. Do you know what I mean?

Like she had to have this pointed out to her. After, you know, it's, it's like she said, no it's not, that's definitely not – It's like – it sounds ridiculous even saying it now but it's like – that's exactly the climate we grew up in. You know –

The SCHOOLBOYS *perform a mocking dance routine, complete with camp hand gestures and effeminate hair-flicking.*

ALL.
Gays were funny things that you laughed at on TV.
Gays were funny people that were like, they were different to everybody else.
They spoke differently. They kind of like, they held themselves differently.
They had different hair.
It was like, they're not the same as everybody else.

MARK. So it's like, so right from the start at school, I can always remember not really homosexuality being a shameful thing, but I can remember it being a really funny thing. And it was something that you would laugh at people for, er, like –

Two STUDENTS *laugh at* MARK *as he accidentally touches one of the other* BOYS. *They act out a grotesque pantomime of sodomising each other.*

STUDENTS.
Oh, my god, you're going off to bum each other!
Oh my god, you're fucking gonna bum each other!
You and him, you're gonna fucking bum each other
Bum each other to death!

All laugh at this outrageous spectacle.

MARK. Which is really funny, until you realise like, oh, hang on a minute. They might be laughing at me as well.

The school bell rings. TEACHER *enters as the* STUDENTS *rush back to their seats. The* TEACHER *hands out exercise books, glaring sternly at the* STUDENTS *as they continue to mess around.*

There were two of these old, authoritarian figures, who actually in all honesty, were quite nice. They were quite Christian, but they were fucking stupid. They were the Religious Education teachers. I remember they did this attempt at teaching sex education, which was the only time homosexuality had ever been formally discussed in a classroom. Ever.

The TEACHER *writes the words 'SEX EDUCATION' on the blackboard.*

Once, she – the, the, the female partner – was taking our class – we would have been fourteen years old, I remember this clear as anything. She had hair like Margaret Thatcher, big blow-dry, it's not a good look for a classroom full of piss-takers in the first place.

But she would get so frustrated by all this sort of uncontrolled energy in front of her that she tried to be nice. And one of her nice things was this class where she said:

TEACHER. Can everybody write a question they have about sex? I'm going to put it in a bag and then I'll answer it in front of the class.

The STUDENTS *write their questions on torn-out pages, and hand them to the* TEACHER. *She picks one out to read.*

MARK. I swear to God, this woman must have only had sex with one man, her husband. They weren't like nasty people but they didn't know shit about shit about anything. And she stood there, and the first question that came out was –

TEACHER. 'Why doesn't God like gay sex?'

Everyone reacts with gasps and hysterical laughter.

MARK. Literally there's this mystery where it comes from. And she tries to explain – she tries to mount this spirited defence of how anal sex is physically impossible.

TEACHER (*simultaneously*). Anal sex is physically impossible!

MARK. She says:

SCENE TWO: GAYS WERE FUNNY THINGS   29

TEACHER. There's absolutely no way. How could – how can that happen? So it's not that God thinks it's unnatural, it *is* unnatural, that thing was not meant to go there.

The TEACHER *holds out her hands, indicating the impossibility.*

MARK. And she's like, she's measuring this, presumably her husband's penis in front of everyone in the class, and everyone is absolutely, this entire classroom, is pissing themselves. Till someone puts their hand up and says –

STUDENT. But what about, Miss, what about when you go for a massive shit?

MARK. At which point she bursts into tears and leaves the room.

The TEACHER *runs out, crying.*

MARK.
**So it's, it's like, that was my school. Yeah.
That's exactly the climate we grew up in.**

The same dance routine – this time, the SCHOOLBOYS *move the blackboard and seats around to form a new classroom layout.*

ALL.
**Where...
Gays were funny things you laughed at on TV.
Gays were funny people that like – they were different to everybody else.**

**They spoke differently. They kind of like,
they held themselves differently. They had different hair.
It was like,
they're not the same as everybody else.**

The STUDENTS *stare forwards as if watching a TV in class.*

CATHERINE. I remember a teacher, an older woman who we all thought was gay. And I remember one day somebody in my class saying to her –

STUDENT. Miss, how comes you're not married?

CATHERINE. She went –

TEACHER. 'Cause nobody's asked me.

CATHERINE. And then, and everybody went –

ALL. *Awwww.*

TEACHER. Stop it.

CATHERINE. Felt really sorry for her. Um, but no, I didn't know a single, um, I, I didn't, I didn't know a single person that was gay.

The ensemble slide down their chairs and perform a slow and sensual routine.

I remember, um, as I, as sort of in the Sixth Form, starting to be aware of certain things, just being aware of like the odd thing on TV. There, there was a, there was a film I watched called *Lianna,* and it was about, um, a woman in, it was an, an American film. It wasn't really very good at all. And it was about an American woman who was married to a man who was very important. And she went to take a class at, at, er, a university class or something, an evening class. And she fell in love with her, her teacher and they, um, and they had an affair. And I just remember, I almost wanted to just climb through the telly. It was just, erm, the most incredible thing I'd ever, I'd ever seen.

A STUDENT *fires a spitball at* CATHERINE*'s head, snapping her back to the present.*

Um. But no, I mean, as far from school, nothing. That was all, that was all there was, I didn't, um, I didn't know anybody, I didn't talk to anybody.

All rise for this shared choral moment, pacing the stage; alone, but together.

CATHERINE.
Um, but no, I didn't know a single, um, I, I didn't, didn't know a single person that was gay.

MARK.
So it's, it's like, that was my school. Yeah.

CATHERINE.
I was completely and utterly in my own world, and I was frightened.

MARK.
That's exactly the climate we grew up in, where –

ALL.
Um, but no, I didn't know a single, no I didn't didn't, know a single person that was gay,
Didn't didn't know, a single person that was gay,
Didn't didn't know, a single person that was gay.

Gays were funny things you laughed at on TV.
Gays were funny people that like – they were different to everybody else.

Scene Three: Positive Images

The classroom is reorganised into a public library.

A LIBRARIAN *walks the corridors wheeling a set of bookshelves, picking up books and ordering them. Others are scattered about, reading.*

MAYA. When I went to school? Good question. I twigged by about twelve that I was different from the others. But I was very careful to keep that concealed and try to figure my way, figure out a bit more about myself and who I was. And when classmates made gay jokes, whatever, I'd just stay silent. And perhaps being Asian it was easier to get away with not having any signs of a boyfriend – people might have just assumed that my parents wouldn't let me or something. But I think my parents might not have minded if I was *slightly* more interested in boys at that point (*Laughs.*) …it took them a little bit of time to become fully affirming.

Back then you know, there was very little visibility in the media. But then, as time went on, you gradually began to see people in silhouette who would talk about their experiences, or with their back to camera. Then finally people would appear in actuality and you know, you could actually see them, and using their own names. And in between the tragic stories there might just be something that was a little bit less tragic.

Archive images of various campaigning materials are projected as MAYA *speaks – the logo for the Positive Images campaign, the cover of a book called* The Playbook for Kids About Sex, *posters publicising a 'Smash the Backlash' demonstration.*

I initially became involved with Haringey Council as a member of the Lesbian and Gay Sub-committee. And at that time in the 80s, there was an increased awareness of the importance of equal opportunities, particularly in Labour-run local authorities.

So as part of that, we were pushing for greater equality for what would've been described as lesbians and gays, though in practice it would also have included bisexual and trans people. Many of the measures then might seem pretty modest now, but at the time it was all seen as really subversive.

So it all started when one of the unit staff wrote to headteachers in the borough flagging up the importance of promoting positive images of lesbians and gays in schools. And the headteachers went crazy. (*Loudly.*) 'How dare you, some guy in the lesbian and gay unit, tell us what to do in our schools?'

Someone in the library shushes MAYA. *She briefly apologises, then returns to the audience.*

But what really kicked everything off was this one book.

The TEACHER *points at a library book in the* LIBRARIAN's *hand.*

TEACHER. Excuse me – what's that one?

LIBRARIAN. Oh that has just come in –

MAYA. There was literally only one or two copies of it, kept in the Inner London Education Authority library.

SCENE FOUR: JENNY LIVES WITH ERIC AND MARTIN 33

LIBRARIAN. It's Danish, it's just been translated. It's actually about –

TEACHER. I'm looking for something for my year ones.

MAYA. And it's not even a very interesting book, to be honest. It had these black and white, documentary-style pictures.

TEACHER. *Jenny Lives with Eric and Martin.*

The TEACHER *turns out to the audience, addressing them as if they are young children.*

Shall we have a read?

Scene Four: Jenny Lives with Eric and Martin

The picture book comes to life in the style of a piece of children's theatre, narrated by the TEACHER. *Her narration is sung-through, in a Mary Poppins-style voice.*

TEACHER.
This is Jenny. She is five.

JENNY *enters – she is played by a male performer, in a blonde wig.*

This is Jenny's dad. He is called Martin.

MARTIN *enters and stands with* JENNY. *They smile at each other.*

And this is Eric.

ERIC *enters and joins them, they stand together as if in a family photo.*

He lives with Jenny's dad. Interesting… perhaps they're brothers?

MARTIN *and* ERIC *give each other a knowing look.*

Well, **Jenny, Martin and Eric live in a little house in Denmark.**

Over the course of the rest of the song, the actors playfully recreate photographs from the book, in a stylised dance sequence. They use the gym platforms and benches as the furniture in Jenny's house.

Martin usually collects Jenny from school. Today he collects her earlier because they're going to make a cake for Eric's birthday.

They have a lot to do. It is late and everything must be ready for when Eric comes home. Jenny helps to whip the cream. Oh, Jenny, you've got it on your cheek, you mucky, mucky girl.

They lay the table in the garden. Martin cuts some flowers from the big lilac bush. Quite a feminine pursuit.

They hide in the house until Eric comes home. They stay quiet as mice and then they sing:

He's so surprised! He claps his hands, and they give him kisses. Oh – how, Scandinavian.

They have a party! They eat cake and then they have to tidy up –

MARTIN *and* ERIC *speak to each other with sudden naturalism – a domestic scene at the kitchen sink.*

MARTIN. Where do you think you're going?

ERIC. I'm going to do the dishes.

MARTIN. No, you're not, it's your birthday.

ERIC. I know if I don't do them you'll get grumpy with me later.

TEACHER. See, if the mother was home tonight she'd just get it done.

TEACHER.
Time passes too quickly, and suddenly, it's night time.

And they all say goodnight, and go to bed.

It is Saturday! Jenny opens her eyes. Everything is quiet.

SCENE FOUR: JENNY LIVES WITH ERIC AND MARTIN

She peeks through the curtains – and yes, the sun is shining. How lovely!

She tiptoes into the bedroom.

JENNY *is in bed with her two dads, snuggling and yawning – an intimate, family image.*

TEACHER.
Sorry… I think there's a mistake here. It says Jenny **tiptoes into 'the bedroom'**, but whose?

The TEACHER *turns and sees the three of them in bed together. Horrified, she walks straight into the bedroom, and starts trying to lift their bedsheet to see what's happening.*

TEACHER. Ugh! what's going on?

MAYA. And this is the bit everybody hated.

TEACHER. Do you mean to tell me that you're – ?

MARTIN. Just waking up, yeah. How did you – ?

TEACHER. Homosexuals?

MARTIN. Well, yes.

MAYA. Because it was two men, you know, in bed, and they weren't wearing tops.

TEACHER. And here you are – naked –

MARTIN. I have got underwear on –

TEACHER. Absolutely stark, testicle –

MARTIN. I'm sorry?

TEACHER. No doubt erect.

MARTIN. Jenny, why don't you go and make some breakfast, darling?

TEACHER. It's an orgy.

MARTIN. Excuse me?

TEACHER. A full-blown orgy, between two sick perverts and a child!

MARTIN. That is disgusting.

TEACHER. It is.

MAYA. You know, it was seen as like, you know, the worst thing ever, almost like, like –

MAYA *and* TEACHER. Child pornography.

MAYA. And then... all fucking hell broke loose.

Scene Five: Ordinary Mums and Dads

The gym platforms are arranged to show the steps outside a school.

PARENTS *are gathered, waiting for their children.*

PETER*'s song and the* PARENTS*' chorus has the sound of a Billy Bragg-style protest anthem.*

PETER.
When I was a boy – not so long ago – who would have thought life was going to change so much? That we would have to fight like this?

MAYA. After the book was found, the right-wing press got hold of it and caused this huge panic among local parents.

PETER *throws a newspaper down on the steps to show the other* PARENTS *which they pass between them, horrified.*

PETER.
Just to safeguard common decency?

MAYA. It was like kicking a hornet's nest. They just awoke this pure terror in people, this idea that something was being forced on them.

PETER.
**Parents around here have been scared.
But together, we can fight.**

PARENT 2. What's this? What's happened now?

SCENE FIVE: ORDINARY MUMS AND DADS 37

PARENT 1. 'Classroom corrupters.' Look at this. 'Lefties Spread Child Sex Poison.'

PARENT 2. Child sex poison? Give it here.

PETER.
Parents around here have been scared.
But together, we can fight.

PETER *addresses the other* PARENTS, *reading them the constitution of his new Parents' Rights Group.*

The aims of the Parents Rights Group shall be to advance the moral education of children. By preventing Haringey Council from introducing the teaching of homosexuality as an acceptable alternative and the teaching of positive images of gays and lesbians. We shall resist such a policy by every legal means at our disposal.

The PARENTS *are galvanised by his speech.*

PARENT 1 *and* PARENT 2.
We shall resist,
We shall resist!

PETER.
Isolated anger can be frightening for parents,
it's so lonely, so exposed, and you wonder if it could rebound on your children.

PARENT 1.
He's a freedom fighter of the angry suburbs.

PARENT 2.
A folk hero for innocence.

PARENTS.
But together, we can fight.
We're the freedom fighters of the angry suburbs,
The folk heroes for innocence,
and together we can fight!

PETER. Our constitution has had an explosive and emotive chain-reaction of support. My phone has been constantly ringing with callers, other angry and anxious parents – parents who are asking:

The PARENTS *stand on their raised gym platforms, calling out to the audience.*

PARENTS.
Where are all the ordinary mums and dads?
Come on, let's hear your voice!
If we don't make a fuss now, these things will keep happening. Are you happy about it?

The PARENTS *rearrange the furniture to form the inside of a community centre – a planning meeting for the Parents' Rights Group.* PARENTS *busily paint placards for a demonstration. These have slogans like 'HARINGEY MOTHERS SAY NO TO GAY CLASSES' and 'LET PARENTS DECIDE'.*

MAYA. I can remember one or two of the people who were very vocal in that group. Who started the school strikes, the rallies, who you'd hear quoted in the media –

PARENT 1. What they want to do with our children is unreal. My two daughters have instructions from me that if the subject of gays and lesbians comes up they have my full permission to leave the classroom, go to the nearest telephone and contact me.

MAYA. There were actually a very mixed set of people, who held this loose kind of alliance. Religious fundamentalists, people from the far right. There would also have been some Black parents, because it was made out that this was some kind of attack on the Black family, and on communities of colour more broadly.

PARENT 2. My daughter Nikki told me she had been taken out of her maths class specially so that a lesbian could tell her how to do it and where to meet lesbians.

PETER. What?

PARENT 2. She told her, 'Don't worry. I won't touch you. I only go for older women.'

SCENE FIVE: ORDINARY MUMS AND DADS 39

PARENT 1. Oh my god, that's awful.

PARENT 2. I can't go into any more detail. I'm too embarrassed. How can it be normal?

PARENT 1. It's not.

PETER. Not normal at all.

PARENT 2. I am grateful to this country.

PARENT 1. Of course!

PARENT 2. But I am responsible for my daughter. I have to see that she grows up to be a normal and happy child.

The PARENTS *set off for their demonstration at the Haringey Civic Centre.*

PETER.
If the council loonies think we're going to fade away, they're wrong,

ALL.
So wrong!

PETER.
'Cause we've begun to fight.
And the battle lines are drawn.

MAYA. So in response to that pressure, the Positive Images group formed to counter some of the myths that were being pedalled. There were some really turbulent council meetings.

The PARENTS *rearrange the set to form the Council Chamber of Haringey Civic Centre – a council meeting is taking place.* MAYA *sits on one side, representing the Positive Images group, and the Parents' Rights Group sit on the other.*

The PARENTS *roar their rousing chorus, overpowering* MAYA.

PARENTS.
Where are all the ordinary mums and dads?
Come on, let's hear your voice!
If we don't make a fuss now, these things will keep happening. Are you happy about it?

PETER. Now listen up, everybody. I have a dog.

MAYA. Where is this going?

PETER. And the other day, my son was taking our dog for a walk. And it's a boy dog. And the boy dog happened upon another boy dog and they did, well, something that two boy dogs don't generally do.

PARENT 2. No!

PETER. Yes! And my son said, I don't know why they're doing this, they're two boy dogs. And two teenage girls standing nearby said, 'Those dogs must have gone to a Haringey school!'

The PARENTS *laugh and cheer.*

MAYA. Okay, yes, very good.

PETER. This council is becoming a national joke – but d'you know what? Parents aren't laughing.

MAYA. Haringey is merely moving forward on a Labour manifesto pledge, adopted as council policy, to educate children about the world around them.

PARENT 2. Is it true that the Education Service is planning to send every child a copy of this book – this *Janet Lives with Eric and Martin*?

MAYA. I'd love to know where you think the council has the resources to send eighty thousand children a copy of a book.

PARENT 1. Are you a mother?

MAYA. I don't see why that's relevant.

PARENT 2. Answer the question.

MAYA. No, as it happens. No, I'm not.

PARENT 1. Then what gives you the right to decide what our children are taught? You don't know the first thing about children.

PARENT 2. Sex education must be taken out of the hands of extremist councillors like you.

SCENE FIVE: ORDINARY MUMS AND DADS

MAYA. This actually has very little to do with sex.

PARENT 1. It's always about sex!

PETER. Thank you!

MAYA. Look, as I have said, the Education Service is delivering on a party commitment to make sure that all types of people are treated fairly in the curriculum –

PETER. Then hold a referendum on the issue!

PARENT 2. Yes!

PETER. Ask us, do parents want positive images of lesbians and gays in schools? Otherwise, we'll be outside those school gates every day, with our kids safely at home.

PARENT 2. Frankly I don't feel safe with them going in anymore.

PARENT 1. No, me neither.

MAYA (*to the audience*). We were in a far weaker position because we were only able to use rational arguments. Most of the debate wasn't rational at all. That was the strength of the Parents' Rights Group – somehow they could tap into these hidden fears.

The PARENTS *move closer to* MAYA *and begin to physically intimidate her. One* MOTHER *circles her threateningly, and ends up with her hands around* MAYA's *throat.*

PARENTS.
**Where are all the ordinary mums and dads?
Come on, let's hear your voice!
If we don't make a fuss now, these things will keep happening.
Are you happy about it?**

MAYA. At the end of one council meeting this woman from the Parents' Rights Group, she had her hands around my throat, and she was screaming and spitting,

PARENT 1. You can't make my daughter be a lesbian!

MAYA. I'm not interested in making your daughter a lesbian!

PARENT 1. Of course you are. You can't reproduce so you have to recruit our kids.

PETER.
When I was a boy not so long ago
Who would have thought life was going to change so much?
That we would have to fight like this just to safeguard common decency?
Parents around here have been scared –

PARENTS.
We shall resist! We shall resist!

The PARENTS, *in a frenzy, pull books from the shelves and throw them across the room to each other, ripping them up. They knock over furniture, and try to attack* MAYA *who runs from them. A whirlwind of chaos surrounds her as she addresses the audience.*

MAYA. People burned this book, um, you know, on the steps of, of town halls and in public almost like a, a kind of ritual burning or something.

People were kind of whipping, whipping each other up, round and round. Um, so I don't, I don't think you can sort of blame maybe one, one particular group or person for it, but, but they kind of fed off each other. And really, you know, the panic was just kind of like almost like a whirlpool or a whirlwind, just kind of getting bigger and bigger and stronger and stronger until –

Scene Six: The Act – Committee Stage

Amidst the frenzy, the school benches, library shelves and gym platforms have been rearranged to form the two opposing sets of benches of the House of Commons.

SCENE SIX: THE ACT – COMMITTEE STAGE

This debate is the Committee Stage of the bill in parliament that will eventually become Section 28. Various MPs sit across from one another.

Archive photographs of Westminster are projected, alongside the words 'Local Government Act 1986 (Amendment) Bill: An act to refrain local authorities from promoting homosexuality'.

SPEAKER. Dame Jill Knight!

DAME JILL KNIGHT. Would it be in order, Mr Speaker, to speak on the bill as a whole?

SPEAKER. Certainly the honourable Lady may do that. The bill has only two clauses.

DAME JILL KNIGHT. Thank you, Mr Speaker.

Throughout DAME JILL KNIGHT*'s speech, she is spurred on by her supporters and heckled by her opponents. They rise as they shout out, and frequently talk over her. Their staccato movements of exaggerated hand gestures, arm-folding and foot-tapping reflect familiar images of bored, angry and unruly MPs in the commons.* DAME JILL KNIGHT*'s sung phrases and words are used for emphasis.*

DAME JILL KNIGHT.
This bill came into being for a very good reason!

GOVERNMENT. Hear hear!

DAME JILL KNIGHT.
It is before the Committee because there is **evidence in shocking abundance**
that **children in our schools, some as young as five years**,
are frequently being encouraged into
homosexuality and lesbianism.

OPPOSITION. Ridiculous!

OPPOSITION. Rubbish!

DAME JILL KNIGHT.
I shall quote only a few examples.
First, there is a publication called ***The Playbook for Kids About Sex*** –

DAME JILL KNIGHT *picks up the various books she is describing, which are strewn across the floor from the chaos of the previous scene.*

GOVERNMENT. Revolting.

DAME JILL KNIGHT.
written for young children and presented in the type of colour and line drawings that would **appeal to a child.**

OPPOSITION. Oh come on.

DAME JILL KNIGHT.
In fact, it is the most frightening piece of propaganda –

OPPOSITION. Propaganda?

DAME JILL KNIGHT.
against children.
A book called *The Milkman's On His Way*.
I shall not shock the House by quoting from it –

GOVERNMENT. Please don't!

DAME JILL KNIGHT.
but, in explicit terms, it describes intercourse between a sixteen-year-old boy and his adult male lover.

GOVERNMENT. Booo!

DAME JILL KNIGHT.
Recently, the Lesbian and Gay Development Unit of Haringey Council made a video called

'How to Become a Lesbian in Thirty-five Minutes.'

OPPOSITION. Did they?

GOVERNMENT. Outrageous!

DAME JILL KNIGHT.
It was shown to mentally handicapped girls. Another book called

Jenny Lives with Eric and Martin –

OPPOSITION (*exasperated*). Ohhhhh...

SCENE SIX: THE ACT – COMMITTEE STAGE

DAME JILL KNIGHT.
that has been the subject of a great deal of public protest.

OPPOSITION. Not this again!

DAME JILL KNIGHT.
It is terrifying to me that local councils have been promoting that kind of stuff.

OPPOSITION. Promoting?

DAME JILL KNIGHT.
There is a pile of filth and it is shocking –

GOVERNMENT. Filth!

DAME JILL KNIGHT.
when one considers it is all paid for by the rates.

OPPOSITION. Hear hear!

OPPOSITION. That is a lie!

DAME JILL KNIGHT.
If anyone doubts that, why did the children's parents complain? When those parents complained, why were they subjected to **such vicious treatment**? **I cannot think it right –**

MR PIKE. Will the honourable Lady give way?

DAME JILL KNIGHT.
No, I am in the middle of a sentence.

I cannot think it right that parents who complained about what was being done to their children at school should have been kicked and spat upon.

GOVERNMENT. Abused!

OPPOSITION. What?

OPPOSITION. When?

DAME JILL KNIGHT.
If their children had not been treated in the way that I have described, the parents would not have complained.

GOVERNMENT. Hear hear!

DAME JILL KNIGHT.
One of the things that has impressed me –

MR PIKE. Is it true?

DAME JILL KNIGHT. The honourable Gentleman asks whether it is true. If it is not true, why did the parents complain? That is the point of the matter.

MR HOLLAND. Will the honourable Lady give way?

DAME JILL KNIGHT. I will give way to the honourable Member for Burnley because he asked me first.

MR PIKE.
Will the honourable Lady give evidence to support her claim?

Does she recognise that the Clause goes way beyond the protection of children?

**Will she also accept that, if the protection of children is the main cause for concern, we must give the same protection to children from the threat from heterosexual abuse.
Which is far more common and a bigger threat.**

OPPOSITION. Hear, hear!

GOVERNMENT. Sit down, man!

DAME JILL KNIGHT. The Clause has nothing to do with criminal abuse. The Clause attempts to stop what has been happening to children.

Various MPs stand to interject.

I will not give way. I want to get on; I do not wish to make a long speech.

**It is important that the House should understand that the Bill
in no way attacks the rights of adult people
to live their own lives in their own way.
It is a free country.**

OPPOSITION. Is it?

SCENE SIX: THE ACT – COMMITTEE STAGE

DAME JILL KNIGHT.
Many homosexuals live their lives totally within the law and would no more think of **molesting little boys** –

OPPOSITION. Jesus!

DAME JILL KNIGHT.
Than a normal heterosexual would think of **molesting little girls**.

OPPOSITION. Really?

DAME JILL KNIGHT.
Nothing in the Bill is aimed at such people. There is all the difference in the world between allowing adults to live in the way in which they consider is right for them and **trying to pervert little children**.

GOVERNMENT. Hear hear!

OPPOSITION. Nonsense!

OPPOSITION. Listen to yourself!

DAME JILL KNIGHT.
Millions outside Parliament object to little children being **perverted, diverted** or **converted** from normal family life to a lifestyle which is desperately dangerous for society and extremely dangerous for them. Any venereologist will say that **syphilis, gonorrhoea and genital herpes are characteristically infections of homosexuals**.

OPPOSITION. Shame!

GOVERNMENT. Quite right!

DAME JILL KNIGHT.
If that were not enough, **we now have the terror of AIDS**.

Scene Seven: Don't Die of Ignorance

DANIEL *emerges, and addresses the audience.*

DANIEL. I was born in 1972. So, I was somebody who was, you know, a teenager during the '80s. Um, so I was, you know, kind of in a way I was the hypothetical child that the government did not want to be gay. But I did try, um, you know, to get a girlfriend, but it didn't take. I was also in denial about being gay as well, myself. So I, at the time I wasn't actively kind of seeking out information.

I was kind of doing the opposite. I was pushing it away. Um, 'cause I, I was scared that if I did seek it out, that someone would know, find out and be like, 'Why are you looking for this?' Or 'Why are you watching this?'

Projected is archival footage of patients being treated for AIDS in hospitals.

DANIEL *sits beside his* MOTHER *and* FATHER *on a bench, who are watching TV.*

But I do remember this documentary programme that my dad and mum and me were watching – I must have been nine or ten at the time – it was saying how gay men were kind of, you know, were most at risk of AIDS and were dying of it, and no one knew how or why. And you know, they were saying they got it from sex, and I remember my mum saying to my dad –

MUM. 'What do gay men... do?'

DANIEL. And my dad said –

DAD. They put it up each other's bums, love.

DANIEL. And my mum kind of went –

MUM. Oooooh!

DANIEL. Like that. And I thought 'Oooh' at the same time. So the first time I heard about AIDS was also the first time I heard about gay sex.

SCENE SEVEN: DON'T DIE OF IGNORANCE 49

MUM (*to* DAD). So, how do they – ? You know what, I'm gonna go put the kettle on.

She walks out awkwardly.

DANIEL. And my mum and I, well, we both discovered what gay men did on the same day.

LB *joins* DANIEL.

LB. I think it would probably have been about maybe '86, '87 –

Projected are clips from the famous 'Don't Die of Ignorance' public-information campaign: an erupting volcano, a gravestone being engraved with the word AIDS, an iceberg in the ocean.

So I was about five or six years old, which seems quite young, but that's when I remember seeing the adverts on the television. There were just tombstones being chiselled and falling over and sort of volcanoes going off in the background. I think things like that. John Hurt's voice, um, it, it made you feel it was a really serious issue.

And so people would say, 'Oh, you're gonna get AIDS' in the playground and things like that. So AIDS was used as a bit of a torment and an insult and it still wasn't really explained... Nobody really, really told us anything.

DANIEL. And I remember in the playground it was literally like – who's going to die of AIDS?

LB. There was no information. I didn't know or understand how you got AIDS. It was just related to sex.

DANIEL. Like a kind of nuclear war thing, like they were the big kind of like disasters –

LB. It was just kind of, you'd see these things on TV and the headlines on the newspapers.

DANIEL. It was either nuclear war or AIDS.

LB. My grandparents read things like the Daily Mail – and it was completely terrifying.

DANIEL. One of them was going to get you, eventually.

Scene Eight: Roll the Dice

The school furniture of desks, blackboard, etc. have been pushed to the back of the room and stacked – as if moved aside for a school disco.

This number is performed as a surreal, 1980's Top of the Pops-*style dance sequence in which the words of tabloid columnists are set to a synth-heavy, Pet Shop Boys or Bronski Beat-style track.*

The JOURNALISTS *perform a repetitive and outlandish dance routine, amidst smoke and flashing lights, each one stepping out from the group to speak to the audience. Projected are trippy, multicoloured visuals of gay men dancing in a club in the 1980s.*

JOURNALIST 1. When I first heard of them they were known as 'bum-boys'. Then it was 'nancy-boys' and 'fancy-boys', and 'pansies' and 'fairies', and 'fruits' and 'fags' and 'faggots', and 'poofs' and 'poofters' and 'queers' and 'gays'.

'Gays' was the name they eventually chose. Now they are reverting to 'queers', but given their disposition, should they not be calling themselves kamikazes?

I ask the question in all seriousness, for they not only seem to have a death wish themselves, but an apparent readiness to inflict death on others.

JOURNALIST 2.
I'm so fed up with this endless talk of AIDS
I am totally and utterly fed up to the back teeth
of hearing AIDS this and AIDS that, rammed down my throat.
My heart goes out to the innocents, especially transfusion victims.
Surely the degenerates, whose perverse actions spread this virus
should be held accountable for infecting innocent people.
The so-called gays!

JOURNALIST 3.
My grandparents' generation called it unhealthy. Little did they realise how right they were. Darwin called it natural selection. Nature's way of eliminating a defect.

JOURNALIST 2.
I think it's time these deviants were told:

CHORUS.
'If you want to roll the dice you've got to pay the price.'
Roll the dice, pay the price
Take the blame for your shame
For this homosexual plague.
Roll the dice, pay the price
Take the blame for your shame
The so-called gays!

JOURNALIST 4.
The Sun says gays must halt the spread of AIDS.
We have always felt pity for people with AIDS ever since the scourge first hit Britain.

At the same time, we have stressed that they only have themselves to blame for their terrible plight.

The term Gay Plague upsets some people, but that effectively is exactly what it is. The overwhelming majority who get AIDS, as Government figures released last night prove, are practising homosexuals who contract the disease through the way they make love.

Only a minute percentage are women – a pathetic group who have the appalling misfortune to have sex with a bisexual man.

It doesn't matter how many AIDS victims shake Princess Di's hand, they have NOT got Royal approval for their abnormal, and to many folk abhorrent, sexual habits.

JOURNALIST 3.
Nancy-boys and fancy-boys, pansies and fairies,
Fruits and fags and faggots
Poofs and poofters, queers and gays.

**Nancy-boys and fancy-boys, pansies and fairies,
Fruits and fags and faggots
Poofs and poofters, queers and gays.**

JOURNALIST 1. The message to every gay in the land is stark:

ALL.
**'If you want to roll the dice, you've got to pay the price.'
Roll the dice, pay the price
Take the blame for your shame
For this homosexual plague.
Roll the dice, pay the price
Take the blame for your shame
The so-called gays!**

The music segues into an organ accompanying a choir, and the ensemble break out of their dance to become a JOURNALIST, *a* VICAR *and his* SON *standing on the top of a mountain. The* VICAR *holds a rifle.*

JOURNALIST 5. A vicar vowed yesterday that he would take his teenage son to a mountain and shoot him if the boy had the deadly disease AIDS.

And to make his point, the Reverend Robert Simpson climbed a hill behind his church and aimed a shotgun at his eighteen-year-old son, Chris. Mr Simpson, sixty-four, said:

MR SIMPSON. Chris would not get closer to me than six yards. He would be a dead man. Even though he is my own child, I would pull the trigger. And that would go for the rest of my family as well as strangers. AIDS is so serious – there is no possible cure.

JOURNALIST 5. Bewildered Chris said:

CHRIS. I don't think I would like Dad to shoot me, but I know there is no chance with AIDS. Sometimes I think he would like to shoot me whether I had AIDS or not.

JOURNALIST 5. But Mr Simpson believes the disease is threatening Britain. He said he would ban all practising homosexuals, who are most in danger of catching AIDS, from taking communion.

MR SIMPSON. I will not let anyone risk the health of my parishioners by allowing them to drink wine from the same chalice.

JOURNALIST 5. Mr Simpson said that in six years' time more than a million people in Britain would have AIDS. He went on:

MR SIMPSON. If it continues it will be like the Black Death. It could wipe out Britain. Family will be against family. Nobody will trust anyone else, and gun law will prevail.

JOURNALIST 5. But the fighting vicar says he has nothing against gays.

Suddenly, the synths and drum machine kick in again and everyone erupts once more into dance.

ALL.
**My grandparents' generation called it unhealthy.
Little did they realise how right they were.
Darwin called it natural selection.
Nature's way of eliminating a defect.**

**Nancy-boys and fancy-boys, pansies and fairies,
Fruits and fags and faggots
Poofs and poofters, queers and gays.
Nancy-boys and fancy-boys, pansies and fairies,
Fruits and fags and faggots
Poofs and poofters, queers and gays.**

**Roll the dice, pay the price
Take the blame for your shame
For this homosexual plague.
Roll the dice, pay the price
Take the blame for your shame
The so-called gays!**

The music slowly rises to a crescendo under the following speech, with the remaining ensemble singing in feral, orgasmic moans. They slowly remove layers of clothing, and simulate grotesque sexual acts with one another.

JOURNALIST 1. With AIDS, practices which people have felt to be immoral have been shown to be lethal.

Drug addicts *are* also affected, but no one is suggesting drug addiction as an alternative lifestyle.

There is little love in their lives and their promiscuity is an attempt to snatch a moment of bliss in physical gratification. They are not preaching a way of life, but a way of death.

They have obtained a greater say in local government, including Ealing and Haringey, and are trying to push their teachings in schools.

And there's a particular worry that children will experiment with homosexual practices, thereby running the risk of catching AIDs. Hence Section 28. If ever a measure were justified by circumstance, this is it.

The pounding music drops out into a more ambient underscore. The feel of a 1980's queer club in the early hours of the morning, with revellers on ecstasy. Slow, sensual dancing as clubbers encounter one another in the darkness and explore each other's bodies. DANIEL *and* LB *take part in this with a mixture of fear and fascination, attraction and repulsion. They address the audience through the undulating bodies.*

DANIEL. Erm, so homosexuality and AIDS were always linked together in my brain, right from the very outset really. So there was always this fear that if I did ever have sex I was going to get AIDS and die in a terrible way. And also in a way that people would hate me for it.

LB. I was terrified of having sex. I didn't know or understand how you got AIDS. It was just related to sex. And then that just made me terrified of having sex my whole life. I didn't lose my virginity until I was twenty-one with my girlfriend. And even then I was just terrified because she'd obviously been with people in the past. So I, it was sort of seen as a gay disease. And I think that's something that I grew up with, but I didn't really understand how that related to my, myself.

DANIEL. Um, and it did make me incredibly anxious, you know, all the way through, um, my teenage years. And then when I started having sex erm… The first time I did get a, an HIV test. Um, I remember the doctor saying to me, you know, well, if you've got it, it's a death sentence, um, in a very kind of matter of fact way, very kind of cold way. And then I had to wait, I think, two weeks to get the results back, which were just awful.

'Cause that, you know, you're kind of thinking, am I gonna get this death sentence in two weeks? And I'm still a teenager, you know, I, you know, it's too young to be thinking of, of dying really. Then I got the results back and it was negative. Um, you know, I just burst into tears because I just, all this kind of emotional fear had been welling up in me. Then, and I remember I sort of, you know, had a couple, few days of feeling really happy and then thinking, but this isn't over, this is just the start of it. I've got to go through this every single time. It's never gonna be over.

Scene Nine: The Act – Commons Debate

The Commons is re-formed with the gym platforms and benches.

The sudden, disorienting snap from the club to Parliament means some of the politicians are still in a state of semi-undress, straddling one another, etc. They gradually find the formation of the Commons, with the government on one side and the opposition on the other.

MR HUGHES.
The debate about the new section, as set out in Clause 28, raises many questions of definition.

GOVERNMENT. Definition?

MR HUGHES.
There is no definition in the Bill of the words '**promotion**', '**acceptability**', '**pretended**' or '**family**'.

GOVERNMENT. It's perfectly clear!

OPPOSITION. It is not!

MR HUGHES.
Subsection (1)(b), if unamended, would read as follows:

'A local authority shall not... **promote** the teaching in any maintained school of the **acceptability** of homosexuality as a **pretended family relationship**.'

MRS ELAINE KELLETT-BOWMAN.
Hear, hear.

MR HUGHES.
The honourable Member says, '**Hear, hear**'.

MRS ELAINE KELLETT-BOWMAN. I do, yes.

MR HUGHES.
It is unacceptable to prevent the teaching that other people's relationships be accepted by all civilised adults, whatever their personal views of the rightness or wrongness of those relationships.

MRS ELAINE KELLETT-BOWMAN.
It depends on what one means by 'civilised'. I do not regard the practice of sodomy or buggery as being civilised.

OPPOSITION. Oh, come on now!

MR HUGHES.
I am not asking the honourable Lady to regard those practices, or any others, as **civilised**.

OPPOSITION. Ha!

MR HUGHES.
I am merely asking her to live in England in **1987** where, just as in **1887**, or **1787**, **those practices go on**.

OPPOSITION. Exactly!

MR HUGHES.
From the beginning of time there have been, are, and will be people who are homosexual, living in such relationships, sometimes with children.

SCENE NINE: THE ACT – COMMONS DEBATE

MRS ELAINE KELLETT-BOWMAN.
Disgusting.

MR HUGHES.
I defend the honourable Lady's right to think that it is
disgusting –

GOVERNMENT. It is!

MR HUGHES.
But I do not defend her right, on behalf of a minority
Government, to legislate to pretend that it does not exist.

MRS ELAINE KELLETT-BOWMAN.
Disgusting.

MR HUGHES.
If the honourable Lady made an effort to inform herself,
she would realise that these things are not **encouraged or
discouraged by teaching that they should be accepted** – just
as other things that she might not like are accepted.

MRS ELAINE KELLETT-BOWMAN.
Disgusting.

SPEAKER. Mr Chris Smith!

MR SMITH.
The difference between the way in which the originators of the
Clause say that they want it to be applied and the **likely impact
of the Clause** reveals the real motives of **those who have
introduced it.**

GOVERNMENT. And what are those?

MR SMITH.
Those motives have now come into the open.

GOVERNMENT. Go on!

MR SMITH.
Both in Committee and on the Floor of the House, some things
have **become sayable** which were **not sayable** two or three
years ago, and that **worries me profoundly**.

OPPOSITION. Hear, hear!

GOVERNMENT. Oh, does it?

MR SMITH.
The climate has changed. There is **more intolerance now** than there was **five or ten years ago**. **The House cannot have failed to notice** that last Saturday there was **an arson attack on the offices of the *Capital Gay* newspaper**.

MRS ELAINE KELLETT-BOWMAN. Quite right too.

OPPOSITION. What was that?

MR HUGHES.
On a point of order, Mr Speaker. I heard the **honourable Member for Lancaster** say that it was **quite right that *Capital Gay* should have been fire** —

MR SPEAKER. Order. I heard nothing.

MRS ELAINE KELLETT-BOWMAN. No I am quite prepared to affirm that it is quite right that there should be an intolerance of evil.

The ensemble swirl around each other, furious and disgusted as tensions threaten to boil over.

ALL (*interrupting*).
Hear, hear.

MR SMITH.
The climate has changed. There is **more intolerance now, than there was** –

MRS ELAINE KELLETT-BOWMAN.
I do not regard the practice of sodomy or buggery as being civilised.

MR HUGHES.
On a point of order, Mr Speaker –

ALL.
Five or ten years ago The House cannot have failed to notice that –

MR SMITH.
Last Saturday there was an arson attack –

MR HUGHES.
On a point of order, Mr Speaker –

ALL.
Disgusting!

Scene Ten: Tennessee Williams

The blackboard is moved to opposite one of the rows of benches, re-forming MARK*'s classroom.*

MARK. When I did my A-levels, one of my A-level texts was *A Streetcar Named Desire* by Tennessee Williams. Er, and from the first time that I read *Streetcar Named Desire*, I was like, this has absolutely blown my mind.

It's so like – it's like, it's so *gay*, it's so like, she is the gayest character ever written, er, I, er. And actually, weirdly, like Tom Wingfield and *Glass Menagerie*, I didn't sort of, like, connect with that sort of, sensitive poet gay. I didn't kind of associate with them. But the fucking drunk one that will sleep with anyone? I was like, I get her, you know what I mean?

That's like, she really makes *sense*, even though it's like, I've thought, you know, she's – ostensibly she is a gay man. Isn't she, Blanche DuBois? It's like, that's who he's written as himself really, hasn't he?

But when we sat down to read this – so the first thing we did was watch the fucking Marlon Brando film of it. Like, oh, Jesus Christ. Be still, my beating heart. This is the most amazing thing I've ever seen. Like, it literally blew my mind from like, you know, I can remember that like from the first fucking time I saw it, I understood it straight away, him. Whoa. You know, like, my God – who is that person?

And where it's like, it's just, the whole thing was just incredible. So we watched the film and then the teacher made this sort of quiet, lovely sort of, like, little impassioned speech. And she said –

He addresses the class as his teacher.

'I dunno if any of you know, but at the moment there's this thing going through parliament called Clause 28. And I'll be perfectly honest with you, if it gets through, if it happens, then we probably won't be able to teach this fucking play.'

The SCHOOLKIDS *react variously: shocked, amused, bored.*

And she's waving it in her hand. And she's like, 'Because the whole thing about this is, and I'm going to tell you now, because next year I might not be able to tell people, Tennessee Williams was gay and he's writing about his gay experience.' And I'm sitting there like, 'Okay… So *that's* why I love her. That now makes sense.'

But yeah she went into this whole, lovely sort of little, quiet impassioned speech and it was like that's, that's really incredible.

Scene Eleven: The Act – Lords Debate

CHARLOTTE *and* SARAH *come forward. As they speak, they dress in their 'Stop the Clause' T-shirts once again.*

CHARLOTTE. We knew something had to be done, because the pressure was building and the press were feeling freer to be more and more homophobic.

SARAH. Yeah.

CHARLOTTE. So, attacks were going up, you know, attacks against lesbians. I think they really fanned the flames of hatred. Um, and women were losing custody of their children. So yeah, the pressure was absolutely appalling.

SCENE ELEVEN: THE ACT – LORDS DEBATE

SARAH. But you just couldn't get on the news about it. It was like this incredibly terrible, awful discriminatory thing that was happening, and yet you couldn't get it on the telly. You couldn't get it anywhere.

CHARLOTTE. There was no platform. We had to make our own platforms for things to get talked about and to be in the news because nobody, um, you know – I think we felt there was no other way for us to get it out there.

SARAH. Yeah.

CHARLOTTE. So, it was the final vote in the Lords.

LORD MASON *sits on a bench in front of the blackboard, and silently makes a speech to the House of Commons as* CHARLOTTE *and* SARAH *continue.*

CHARLOTTE. We only planned it literally the day before, or the night before. I was in the public gallery listening to the debate and wondering what we could do. And by that time, they were broadcasting the House of Lords, you know, on the television, er, the debates.

SARAH. And the Lords felt, as did the Commons, they felt empowered to say really, really deeply offensive and bigoted things. And nobody seemed to care that this, this language was being used in a public arena.

CHARLOTTE. And this was both Tory and, and Labour Lords. Wasn't it? It wasn't confined to the usual suspects. And it was extreme. But that licence to the space that was created, where they felt able to do that, had been built over time. And nobody was saying, 'this is outrageous!'

SARAH. So it needed for somebody to do something.

SARAH *and* CHARLOTTE *pick up and examine various pieces of furniture, reorganising the layout of the space as they strategise their next move. They look up at the light fittings.*

LORD MASON.
Loony-left Labour councils, mainly in London, have abused their powers.

They took no account of the views of the majority of ordinary people.

They launched and financed programmes to aid and abet homosexuality, lesbianism and other minority causes until they became the laughing-stock of the nation.

Someone has to restrain that promotion before it becomes widespread!

CHARLOTTE. I was looking at the lights hanging down from the ceiling and thinking… cool. We could maybe, like, swing on those lights.

SARAH (*unconvinced*). Hmmm.

CHARLOTTE. I don't think frankly they would have held anybody's weight, but yeah, that's where the idea came from.

So there was quite a big group of us. There were ten of us actually, um, that travelled up the next day and we brought a washing line on Clapham Market and got on the bus and uh, all ten of us crowded into the, into the, the lobbies, outside the House of Lords.

SARAH. I had the washing line in my jacket.

They walk past a SECURITY GUARD *who eyes them suspiciously, then* LORD MONKSWELL *signs them into a sign-in sheet.*

CHARLOTTE. We walked straight through the alarm thing, because of course the washing line didn't set that off. Then a Lord came along, Lord Monkswell. Um, and he offered to sign four of us into the guest gallery. Cheers, mate! (*To* SARAH.) You go that way!

SARAH *and* CHARLOTTE *attach two school benches to the tops of two gym platforms, creating ramps that they both climb up. As they climb, they loudly heckle* LORD MASON *below.*

LORD MASON.
Commentators have been drawing our attention to the concern

SCENE ELEVEN: THE ACT – LORDS DEBATE

> **about the high profile**
> **of the raucous minority of homosexuals –**

CHARLOTTE. We'll show you raucous!

> LORD MASON.
> **and there is a lot of truth in what they say.**

SARAH. No, there isn't!

> LORD MASON.
> **In *The Times* last week:**

CHARLOTTE. This is hate speech!

LORD MASON *reads from a copy of* The Times.

> LORD MASON.
> **'Many homosexuals bear a heavy responsibility**
> **for the current nasty atmosphere**
> **and for the future threat.'**

SARAH. What threat?

> LORD MASON.
> **'It is they who have deliberately and provocatively**
> **adopted a militantly high public profile – '**

CHARLOTTE. Hardly!

> LORD MASON.
> **'who have flaunted their sexuality – '**

SARAH. Where?

CHARLOTTE. As if!

> LORD MASON.
> **'who have aggressively paraded their lifestyle – '**

CHARLOTTE. What, by living our lives?

> LORD MASON.
> **'and who seem to enjoy the resultant shock and**
> **relish the public distaste.'**

SARAH. The distaste is mutual mate!

CHARLOTTE. Bastard!

LORD MASON.
'They are entitled to do this.
But when they do it they should not expect to be
liked, **loved**, or even **respected** as a result.'

CHARLOTTE. Booooooo!

SARAH. Wanker!

LORD MASON.
'The raucous minority must learn to live with this Clause and the Act.'

SARAH *and* CHARLOTTE *look at each other across the floor, from their high vantage points.*

SARAH. We weren't going to do the action if they voted against, uh, Section 28.

CHARLOTTE. No.

SARAH. The press afterwards were saying you were gonna do it anyway but no, we weren't gonna do it anyway. 'Cause there's always, there's always that kind of slight thing, you know, 'you're a troublemaker'.

CHARLOTTE. Right.

SARAH. Isn't it?

CHARLOTTE. Yeah, yeah.

SARAH. 'You're not rational.' But we were waiting to see which way the vote went.

The LORD SPEAKER *enters and addresses the Commons, revealing the outcome of the vote.*

LORD SPEAKER. The question is whether Clause 28, as amended, shall stand part of the Bill. My Lords, they have voted.

Contents, 202.

Not contents, 122.

The contents have it.
The contents have it!

SCENE ELEVEN: THE ACT – LORDS DEBATE   65

CHARLOTTE. We were just kind of frozen, I think with, like, fear.

SARAH. Yeah, my recollection is that we were kind of going 'ahhhh' and the other women were going 'go on!'

CHARLOTTE. And then... we jumped.

The two activists descend their ramps as if abseiling. They sing rousing, angry slogans as they throw glitter and streamers down on LORD MASON *and the* LORD SPEAKER. *They throw a handmade banner over the blackboard that reads 'STOP THE CLAUSE'.*

SARAH *and* CHARLOTTE.
Shame on you!
Lesbians are angry!
How could you vote for this bill?

It's alright for you, you don't have to live with it!
We will not be silenced!

Chaos onstage as the activists are captured by SECURITY GUARDS *and restrained.*

CHARLOTTE. There was a huge scuffle. And in the scuffle, they arrested, you know, they detained another woman who was nothing to do with the action called Claire. She was a dyke there demonstrating, but she wasn't with us.

The POLICE *detain them with the help of a school bench.*

Grainy, archival footage and photographs of Big Ben and Westminster are projected.

SARAH. They put us in a, they detained us in a, well, a small room, a cell right up by big Ben for several hours. But the police were rather taken with it really because they, they kept coming in and saying –

The two POLICEMEN *reappear from behind the blackboard.*

POLICEMAN. You're on *The Six O'Clock News*! You're on the *Channel Four News*!

SARAH. You know, even the superintendent came in and said:

SUPERINTENDENT. Off the record, that was the most amazing thing I've ever seen in all my years here.

SARAH. And it did get a lot of press. When we got released, we met up with the others and the press were already interviewing some of them outside Westminster. And then we said, 'Well, we'll tell you more of the story… If you go and buy us a drink!'

CHARLOTTE. 'If you buy us twenty Bennies and half a pint.'

SARAH. It's a cheap story, babe. I phoned my dad from the payphone in the back of a pub. And he said to me, 'I think I know where you are.' He was like, he was like, 'I knew it would be you.' In a nice way, you know. So that's how I know it must have been on the telly.

CHARLOTTE. It was, it was!

SARAH. He must have seen it on the evening news.

CHARLOTTE. We didn't calculate it, but it was much, much more important than any of those news headlines, because that was seen by lots of, at the time, quite lonely, isolated, confused, depressed, um, not knowing what to do, feeling weird, young gays and lesbians all over the country –

SARAH. Mmmm.

CHARLOTTE. – sat on the sofa with, you know, with whatever family members. And they may not have said anything to their family members, but since then – haven't they? – they have said to us on various occasions.

SARAH. Yeah.

CHARLOTTE. 'That meant a huge amount to me.'

SARAH. Yes, because they felt someone was –

CHARLOTTE. Fighting for them.

SARAH. Fighting their – yeah. And, it doesn't matter what was said on one particular day in the newspapers, because actually. You know, headlines are there, and then they're gone.

SCENE ELEVEN: THE ACT – LORDS DEBATE   67

CHARLOTTE. Right, Whereas for somebody to just have that little inkling of hope, there's something out there. If I can, if I can find it, there are people out there who will stick up for me. So I, I don't think we had really thought about that aspect of it, but it was the bit of it that I think was actually in the end, the most important.

SARAH. Yes.

CHARLOTTE. It was individuals not feeling alone.

The ensemble all re-enter and sing the Act One finale, inhabiting the various characters they have embodied for each relevant line.

ALL.
**The climate has changed (the climate has changed)
There is more intolerance now, (there is more intolerance now)
Than there was
Five or ten years ago.
The House cannot have failed to notice that**

**The climate has changed
Some things have become sayable
There is more intolerance now
Which were not sayable
The raucous minority must learn to live with this Clause and the Act
That was my school, yeah
Um, but no I didn't know a single um I didn't didn't know a single person that was gay
Live with this Clause and the Act
I was completely and utterly in my own world and I was frightened
Live with this Clause and the Act.**

ACT TWO – AFTER THE ACT

Scene One: Cheated

MARGARET THATCHER *enters in a long, blue trenchcoat, her hair in its characteristic bouffant. She stands behind a podium and addresses the crowd at the 1987 Conservative Party Conference.*

THATCHER. We want education to be part of the answer to Britain's problems, not part of the cause. To compete successfully in tomorrow's world – against Japan, Germany and the United States – we need well-educated, well-trained, creative young people. Because –

**If education is backward today,
National performance will be backward tomorrow.
Our children don't get the education they need
Too often don't get the education they deserve.**

**And in the inner cities – where youngsters must have
A decent education, to have a better future
A decent education, to have a better future**

**They're cheated
Taught society offers no future
Cheated
Opportunity snatched from them
Children
Children who need encouragement
Are cheated of a sound start in life
Yes, cheated! of a sound start in life**

She rips off her trenchcoat to reveal a glittery blue dress and heels. Her speech becomes a riotously camp, cabaret routine as she pole-dances around her podium and generally thrusts and gyrates around the stage – this is Drag Thatcher.

SCENE ONE: CHEATED

Documentary footage of the crowds outside the conference are projected, along with the slogan 'The Resolute Approach'.

**Children who need, to express themselves in English
Are being taught, political slogans**

**And children who need, to count and multiply
learn anti-racist mathematics – whatever that may be.**

**Opportunity, is all too often snatched
by education authorities, and extremist teachers
by hard-left authorities, and extremist teachers.**

THATCHER'*s adoring* FANS *storm the stage and become her backing dancers and vocalists.*

**They're cheated
Taught society offers no future
Cheated
Opportunity snatched from them
Children
Children who need encouragement
Are cheated of a sound start in life
Yes, cheated of a sound start in life**

**Children who need to be taught to respect
traditional moral values
These children are being taught that they have
an inalienable right to be gay**

**Cheated
Taught society offers no future
Cheated
Opportunity snatched from them
Children
Children who need encouragement
Are cheated of a sound start in life
Yes, cheated! of a sound start in life**

THATCHER *meets her* FANS *and shakes their hands. One faints from over-excitement.*

THATCHER. But the key to raising standards is to enlist the support of parents. The Labour left – hard, soft and in-between – they hate the idea that people should be able to choose. In particular, they hate the idea that parents should be able to choose their children's education.

The Conservative Party believes in parental choice.

ALL.
Cheated!

THATCHER *points an accusing finger at her audience, as her* BACKING DANCERS *hold a ludicrous musical-theatre pose.*

The music drops and becomes something more surreal and ethereal, the words 'choice' echoing beneath it. The CROWD *around her slowly deconstructs the image, as someone takes off her wig, another removes her dress and sparkly shoes. Her podium is taken away. Finally, all that's left behind is a performer in a sports bra and shorts.*

A school bench is placed behind her.

Scene Two: A Double Life

1990s. A school gym. Throughout this sequence, CATHERINE *dresses into sports attire.*

CATHERINE. You know, they say you can't be what you can't see. And I wasn't actually that sporty, but I had a huge crush on my own PE teacher, um, who was from Liverpool. Um, so I had this complete fascination with, with the Scouse accent. Um, I was completely obsessed with her, obsessed with all Scouse accents. And I went to do my teacher training in, in Liverpool on the back of that. I also wanted a job where I could wear a tracksuit every day. Um, I, I knew that PE teachers, you know, tended to be gay.

SCENE TWO: A DOUBLE LIFE

I worked so hard to become a PE teacher and becoming a PE teacher was my ambition and it was going to be absolutely fantastic.

But arriving in, into teaching at the same time as Section 28, it was just... I just didn't realise how I would have to literally lead a double life. I literally have to be two people.

I remember Section 28 talked about, um, a 'pretended family relationship'. Um, I was in a pretended family relationship, but when I was at that school, I pretended in lots of ways. You know, I, I, I pretended to live on my own, so nobody asked me any difficult questions. I pretended to be a private person. So nobody said, 'Who are you going on holiday with?' Or 'What did you do at the weekend?' I pretended very quickly to have, er, to have a boyfriend.

And, you know, teaching's a really hard job. Um, and then if you are managing this whole other turmoil underneath saying, 'Oh my God, who's gonna ask me something?' Or you, you, you, you, you're three steps ahead of yourself so that you don't accidentally out yourself.

A nightclub. A group of people dance in slow motion to '90's garage beats. A YOUNG WOMAN *steps forward from the group and makes eye contact with* CATHERINE *as she speaks.*

So I, I remember, um, going down to, um, a gay bar on a Saturday night, in, in Liverpool with my girlfriend and walking in there and standing and talking and I, I could sense somebody looking over, but I didn't, I, you know, it's dark and, and, and anyway, I turned around and I, I saw, um, I saw a girl from my, um, sixth form netball team who, and I didn't know, I just did not, she was with somebody else who I didn't recognise, but I didn't know what else, I just didn't know what to do. Um, she could see that I'd seen her. So I sort of just like raised my bottle in, in, in that direction.

She raises a sports bottle.

The DANCERS *leave.*

Um, and then we left, er, in a hurry and I spent the entire rest of the weekend thinking that when I turned up on a Monday morning to school, that would be it, I would've lost my job. Um, the headteachers would, er, would call me into, to, to the office and, you know, that would be the end of me. And I, I, you know, my parents would be ashamed.

A crowd of SCHOOL KIDS *traipse in, holding drawstring PE bags.*

So Monday morning arrived and I went into school.
I remember like it was yesterday. I had cross country. Um, I set the cross country runners off, um, stood, stood there. And the, um, the student I'd seen in the bar came and stood with me out on the cross country field and she got upset and she said –

STUDENT. I'm really, um, I'm really sorry about Saturday night. You won't tell anybody, will you? I'm, I'm, I'm really, I'm really worried. I think I might be gay. Um, I, I'm, I just, I don't know what to do.

CATHERINE. And instead of, instead of putting my arm around her and saying, 'you know what, it'll be okay, and don't worry about it', I said – (*Addressing the* STUDENT.) 'I don't want to talk about it. You're not gay. Don't be so ridiculous. Imagine how ashamed your mum and dad would be if they found out that you were gay. We must never talk about this again. Back you go into the school building.'

I just felt completely and utterly exposed and terrified to have had that conversation that she clearly needed to have. Um, it would've been career-ending for me. I remember that student. Um, I worry about that student today. Um, I'm ashamed, um, that I let that student down. Um, and you know, I've got, I've, I guess I've got to live with that.

Scene Three: Book Closed

The ensemble change into their PE kits.

LB*'s song has a '90's grunge feel. Its verses are conversational and rhythmically sung, its chorus rising into a full-blown rock concert – as if their repressed emotions are suddenly given space to erupt.*

LB.
So I, um, I grew up in a, um, small village, um, on the outskirts of Guildford. Sort of in between two villages and so it was quite an isolated place.

I was at school during the sort of height of **this kind of period. So really it was just an absence of knowing anything whatsoever. It was like living in a void and looking at people and just thinking –**

LB *looks at the other students.*

I don't really feel like you, I don't really like, understand how I'm supposed to be.

I really wanted to be a boy.

I had to press down a lot of the feelings that I had within me, um, because I felt if anyone actually knew them, that they would reject me.

When I turned sixteen, um, I realised I was attracted to girls and obviously at the time identifying as, um, a lesbian and as a female kind of, because I didn't really have any other options or any other words for my gender
Um, it was just terrifying if I'm honest with you.

It was just like, I don't wanna come out.
You know, and –

SCHOOLGIRLS *changing into their PE kits notice* LB.

STUDENT. What are you looking at?

STUDENT. You looking at her tits?

STUDENT. Oh my god, she was!

LB. I wasn't!

One of the STUDENTS *pins* LB *to the ground.*

STUDENT. Oh, don't she'll start leaking!

STUDENT. D'you want a big, wet fanny in your face?

STUDENT. She does, she does!

STUDENT. Eurgh, she's flooded her basement.

LB. Get off me, get off me!

STUDENT. Ewww, she's actually humping me.

STUDENT. Course she is. She's a lesbian, she'll take what she can get.

STUDENT. Dyke.

LB tentatively picks themselves up from the floor.

LB.

And I was like, that's, you know, **not something that I want** for myself. **And I really remember one day thinking, oh, I, I looked at myself in the mirror and I go, I can't be gay. I've just gotta find myself a boyfriend.**

Um – I'm gonna pull a boy and everything will be fine again.
And I'll just forget about this,
but these like, nagging thoughts just kept coming to my head.
And I thought –

Do you know what, surely we were taught about this in PSE, like Personal Social Education.

LB frantically pulls a textbook out of their PE bag.

So I went and found my PSE like workbook and I went through it and I found the bit that said homosexuality. And it was just one sentence:

One of the SCHOOLGIRLS *voices the PSE Workbook.*

SCENE THREE: BOOK CLOSED

PSE WORKBOOK. 'People who are attracted to people of the same sex.'

She snatches the book away.

LB.

And that was it, book closed. Like, I got nothing else. Um, it was just terrifying if I'm honest with you. It was just like, I don't wanna come out living in a void I can't be gay. I've just gotta find myself a boyfriend.

A football is kicked onstage. The SCHOOL KIDS *begin to play a game of Piggy in the Middle, with* LB *in the middle.*

FELIX. That was the peak of 'gay' being used as a synonym for bad. Um, yeah, gay... like I suppose maybe I think by that point, 'queer' as an insult had kind of been faded out a little bit, and that wasn't used anymore.

FELIX.

It was just, **everything was gay, gay, gay, gay, gay, gay, gay, or poof, poofy gay, gay poof**.

Um, and it was just, it was just using an insult in a way to, um, bring people down, I guess. Um, no one was, certainly when I was there, I don't think anyone was out.

ENSEMBLE.

Gay, gay, gay, gay, gay, gay, gay, or poof, poofy gay, gay poof
Gay, gay, gay, gay, gay, gay, gay, or poof, poofy gay, gay poof

LB.

They did a, um, they did a safer sex workshop at my school, which was quite, I think in a way quite good. And they talked about being under pressure to do drugs and sex and stuff like that.

And then they said something like 'one in ten of you will be gay'. And then people went:

They quickly pass the ball from one person to another in a game of Hot Potato.

ENSEMBLE.
1, 2, 3, 4, 5, 6, 7, 8, 9, 10 – you're gay!

LB. And so then that person would be relentlessly picked on.

The SCHOOLKID *left holding the ball is pointed and laughed at.*

LB.

And that was it, book closed. Like, I got nothing else.
Um, it was just terrifying if I'm honest with you.
It was just like, I don't wanna come out
living in a void
I can't be gay. I've just gotta find myself a boyfriend.

Scene Four: Slightly Odd Behaviour

The sound of an organ playing a hymn or school anthem.

The other STUDENTS *carry out circuit training around the stage – making use of benches, agility tables, the floor to perform abstracted variations of press-ups, bench dips, etc.*

IAN. So I started secondary school in 1990, left in '96. And the grammar school was a really aspirational place to go. Um, very old fashioned. It still had boarders. Still wore caps, school caps, um, and people just a few years above me still told stories of still getting hit with the ruler, and all that kind of thing.

So it was a proper, proper kind of regimented grammar school. So we weren't actually allowed to play football because that was considered common. So we would do rugby in the winter and in the summer we would do swimming and running. Um, very traditional. So every morning for assembly boys on one side girls on another, um, and all of the tutors frog marched in, in their university gowns, um, that kind of a school.

SCENE FOUR: SLIGHTLY ODD BEHAVIOUR

Um, so in the playground there was quite a lot of really unpleasant stuff. Um, so, um, I was quite camp and quite effeminate growing up, um, especially at secondary school. I didn't really, I kind of thought I might be camp or effeminate, but it was certainly pointed out a lot by a lot of people in a way that I didn't understand. Everyone kept telling me that I was gay. I had no idea. I didn't know I was at the time, I didn't understand what the point was – (*Laughs.*) Erm, just thought I'm just being me.

The SCHOOLBOYS *form an intimidating line as they stretch, which* DANIEL *walks past.*

So I remember, um, there was a walk, a horrible walk from school, as everyone has, I think – so from the school gate down to the bus, um, stops. And, um, there was a long alley called 'dark alley', and people used to wait there and spit on me quite a lot, um, and throw things at me, throw things at my bag, um, there was quite often the call of 'Look out, backs against the walls!' ...Um, that sort of thing.

I used to, um, have slightly odd behaviour. I started self-harming. And I used to use it as an opportunity to get out of spaces that I was really uncomfortable in. Um, so there was, there were issues that the school was very much aware of.

So I did, um, I, I struggled quite a lot and after a time, I attempted suicide at school.

I took an overdose at school, at the age of fifteen. I, Um, had a *matron* who – (*Laughs.*) who then sat with me and started talking. She was lovely. Um, but none of it came out in the wash. And they, they didn't know what to do with me. They recommended, um, some counselling sessions.

The counsellor didn't know, hadn't a clue, or potentially wasn't allowed at any point in time to broach the subject with me that I might be there because I might be gay. If somebody had been able to, um, say to me, 'have you ever thought – ? Do you think that the reason you are here is – ?' um, that may, may have been very different.

Scene Five: The Silence is Deafening

The music takes on a more ecclesiastical sound.

LB *steps forward.*

Around them, the gym circuit training continues.

LB. You know, growing up in quite an isolated space with people who are quite conservative, how are you ever gonna find any information? Then stick a, you know, a government policy on the top of that saying you can't say anything...

So there was quite a big church in Guildford. Um, and they kind of had a very groovy, that sounds horrendous, but it was quite a cool youth scene. So they had Christian club nights and Christian gig nights, uh, at some of the local clubs. And I thought, 'oh, well, this is cool.'

But then it started to get quite intense about the whole sex thing.

I told the youth leader, um, one day that I thought I was bisexual and he suggested that I needed to go for some extra meetings.

LB *is handed a skipping rope by their* PE TEACHER, *who watches on.*

Um, and they were like, 'This is really bad. It's really sinful. And you know, I think we need to see if we can change that.'

From their perspective, um, I had demons. So, and they felt that those demons contributed to me having an abnormal sexuality. And so if I was released from those demons, then I could go on to form normal relationships with men.

I thought, well maybe this is my chance to be normal.

They begin skipping – slowly at first, finding a rhythm. The other STUDENTS' *routines follow the same rhythm.*

Um, and there was a guy at the church who led these prayer sessions and he seemed quite a friendly guy, but when they pray over you, it's quite violent. They talk about, you know,

SCENE FIVE: THE SILENCE IS DEAFENING

things being removed from your body and it's quite physical as well.

And it wasn't just me that was going through this.

What we went through you know, you shake, I would talk in tongues. There was a lot of screaming and there was being held down on the floor, uh, holy water being thrown over you. I remember being dragged by my ankles across the carpet and I could hear my friend screaming in the room next to me.

The skipping builds in intensity – a relentless, physically draining activity – and the organ gets louder.

It kind of went on for about two or three weeks and I'd have these prayer sessions that were really long and people knew that they were happening. If you were down in the coffee bar area, you could hear people screaming in the prayer rooms. And I remember coming out of one of these sessions and just being so shaken up and they, they would hold you down until you were retching and sick. And then they'd say that the demon was gone.

They stop skipping, tangled in the rope.

So, yeah, it's kind of something. Um, and I came out these sessions and I remember this other girl that I'd met on, uh, a, um, Christian camp and she was queer. Um, and she said, do you think this is gonna happen to me? Do I have to go through this? And I didn't have an answer for her. And I just felt really sorry for her because she looked grey when she saw me coming down the stairs.

I feel like what dominated me because of Section 28 was fear. And without any information that fear just led me to make this choice that what I needed to do was to change who I was.

So I think the legacy of Section 28 is the silence.

And that silence itself is very, very loud. That sounds like a completely bizarre thing to say. The silence is loud. It's deafening.

The music stops.

Scene Six: The Legacy

The characters address the audience directly, in a stark silence.

CATHERINE. I think with Section 28, you know, it was repealed in 2003 in the UK, actually 2000 in Scotland, but there was no fanfare. fifteen years is a long time to create a culture. And that culture was, you know, I think we're still undoing it now.

IAN. The legacy? Erm, other than a total infringement of human rights... and I'm not a human-rightsy person, which sounds really stupid... A total infringement of human rights, complete and utter suppression, complete and utter denial of enabling somebody to be who they fundamentally are. Yeah. Oh.

He starts to cry.

Sorry. Yeah, um, yeah, it set an infrastructure and a society up that didn't allow you to be who you are. Fundamentally.

MAYA. I think that there's a huge amount to be learned from Section 28 about just hearing one another. I think that can go a long way towards helping to dispel peoples' fears. How can we really start to listen to each other? Maybe it's something about how you introduce certain policies, particularly to do with children, and ensuring parents feel listened to in that process. But also, you know, there is an importance of holding firm where there are key issues of principle. It's being able to find that balance. We can't just go back to saying, 'let's pretend that all these people don't exist, just go away my dear and come back in twelve years'. That's never going to be helpful advice for young people who are trying to discover their identity.

LB. I've been in therapy now since I was thirty-six. Um, and it's been the most helpful thing that I've done, but I just wish the church would have paid for it. I came out as non-binary, when I was about thirty. Like I don't really know that the term for me was something I'd found before. Um, and that's when I realised that my gender was quite more, a lot more nuanced. Then it's just been in the last, maybe three, four years that I've really started to make my voice heard and you know, correct people when they use the, er, wrong pronouns. Becoming your own advocate is something that takes a lot of time and in an environment where there's no information for you to be able to be your own advocate, you can't. But my sexuality and gender isn't something that needs changing. Actually, it just needs affirming. We've got people who are killing themselves, had serious mental health problems and you can't say you want less suicides, less deaths, less bullying on the one hand, and yet on the other hand say someone's gender expression is somehow wrong and can be changed. Because we've tried it the other way. It doesn't work.

CATHERINE. I absolutely think this era that we are in now is really the Section 28 of the trans community. And it feels so important for me to be able to say that today, because with Section 28, there was that sense that, um, as teachers, we couldn't speak up about it. So hats off to all those people that did go on those marches, because we couldn't. We couldn't have our face in, in the local newspaper or be spotted by a parent or a colleague or, or, or a kid from school. So those that did that, that political campaigning, and pointed out the injustice of it when they weren't affected as much as us... I just think I'll be forever grateful.

Scene Seven: The Manchester March

A demonstration in Manchester against Section 28, two weeks after it passed into law. Projected is colourful, grainy archival footage of the march itself.

MARK. That march in Manchester, right after the Clause was voted through. It feels like, it was almost the sort of Ano Domini and Before Christ of, of gay Manchester that day. That's where it all began for that city.

And the thing with growing up gay when it's kind of
associated with shame or whatever, is that you think
everybody disapproves of it, you think everybody is going to
disapprove of you. And then when you see loads of people
and it's not just, it's not just visibility of people that are sort
of gay or lesbian. It's that there's loads of fucking supporters
of that as well.

A STEWARD *marshalls people around the stage, holding
a megaphone, as they rearrange the gym platforms and
benches to form a large stage.*

STEWARD.

Please go round the back of the memorial, to the right-hand-side of the stage, please. There are literally thousands of us here today.

The police estimate it at fifteen thousand –

Cheering.

our estimates are a lot nearer twenty thousand.

Cheering.

This is the biggest demonstration that's been known in Manchester for well over ten years.

MARK. So Albert Square – it was fucking massive. It's like
Manchester's version of Trafalgar Square being absolutely
full. And also not necessarily just of gay people, there were
a lot of socialist workers there, students. Manchester's
a socialist city so – it's not like the Anti-Brexit marches
with yummy mummies, it's like properly aggro, had a
good atmosphere, really camp, quite bristly. But also there
were loads of TV cameras, and every time I saw one I just
ran away in case my mum would see me, like I genuinely
thought I'd be outed on the six o'clock Granada reports. All
my aunties are going to be horrified, calling my mum and
saying, 'Oh my god, he's one of them.' Do you know what I
mean?

STEWARD.

For those of you who are lucky enough to be at the front, there are still banners and people coming into the square.

SCENE SEVEN: THE MANCHESTER MARCH

This is the biggest demonstration that's been known in Manchester for well over ten years.

The crowds bustle around, putting on T-shirts reading 'Stop the Clause' and 'Never Going Underground' and picking up a variety of printed and homemade placards. These have slogans like 'Stop the Clause – One of your children could be gay!' And 'Defend lesbians and gays – fight the bigots now!'

And we're very proud of that.

STIFYN PARRI *and* SUE JOHNSTON, *actors from the soap opera* Brookside, *stand on an elevated gym platform and address the crowds.*

SUE JOHNSTON.
I hadn't intended to speak, I'm not very good without a script. But I have to say something! When I first heard about Clause 28, I thought of Hitler's burning of the books.

And we all know what happened there, and it must not happen here!

CROWD. Stifyn! Stifyn! Stifyn!

STIFYN.
No one piece of legislation and no government is going to force us to go back into the closet!

Cheering.

What makes you think we will go quietly? It is you who now must fear us.

Because who the hell's gonna get a closet big enough for all of us?

MARK. I did do a terrible thing – I actually snuck off that march. I somehow managed to lose Andy, my friend, in Albert Square and followed the path down, and had this thought, as you do when you're sixteen and everything, literally every thought you have, is about sex. I was like –

'Oh my god, this is amazing. I'm never going to see this amount of gay people again in my life. There are so many people here that I could potentially have sex with.'

The benches are re-organised to form a public toilet. The performers begin circling MARK, *staring at him longingly and singing a choral underscore.*

And I knew there was… a cottage, basically. At the top – if you go down Oxford Road, Manchester Polytechnic had a building called the Nelson Mandela building, I was like I could just nip off there see what's going on and you know, cut off the fucking demonstration and the top floor toilets were just, as suspected, given how many people were there, and –

The MEN *in the toilet grab* MARK, *and each other, in a series of suggestive ways in time with the music.*

it was – it was **rampant**.

Absolutely like positively **bacchanalian**.

So they were all kind of like students, they were older and – it was **hot**.

So that's my other memory of that march. So it sort of did its bit for gay education in plenty of ways.

GRAHAM STRINGER, *Leader of Manchester City Council, stands on the platform and gives a speech.*

GRAHAM STRINGER.
First of all, on behalf of Manchester City labour party and the council,
I'd like to welcome everybody from outside Manchester **to Manchester**
and say **what a wonderful demonstration** this is

Cheering.

Yesterday in this square, **there was a demonstration**, not quite as large as this,
around health service issues.

And there is obvious links – people at the moment, in this country, are very concerned about health. They're very

SCENE SEVEN: THE MANCHESTER MARCH

concerned about civil rights.

And we shouldnt make the mistake of thinking that **Clause 28** – the attacks in the national media and the press, on gays **and lesbians** are disassociated.

**The real project that the conservatives are on is to destroy public service,
is to destroy local democracy,
and place the power in the hands of those people, and those organisations, with the most money.**

The reason Clause 28 is **being introduced**, is to divert attention **from their real project
– and to scapegoat, and victimise, and create second-class citizens.**

Manchester City Council and the Labour Party in Manchester, are not prepared to be used to create second-class citizens in this city, or anywhere else.

STEWARD.
Please go round the back of the memorial, to the right-hand-side of the stage, please. There are literally thousands of us here today.

The police estimate it at fifteen thousand –

Cheering.

our estimates are a lot nearer twenty thousand.

Cheering.

This is the biggest demonstration that's been known in Manchester for well over ten years.

GRAHAM *rejoins the crowd, and all the* DEMONSTRATORS *come forward – raising their placards aloft – to chant and sing their defiant protest to the audience.*

This is the biggest demonstration that's been known in Manchester for well over ten years.

What makes you think we'll go quietly?

It is you who now must fear us.

What makes you think we'll go quietly?
It is you who now must fear us.

Stop Section 28
Stop Section 28
Stop Section 28
Stop the Clause!

Stop Section 28
Stop Section 28
Stop Section 28
Stop the Clause!

No one piece of legislation and no government
is going to force us to go back into the closet!

Because who the hell's gonna get a closet
Big enough for all of
Big enough for all of
Big enough for all of us?

End.

www.nickhernbooks.co.uk

@nickhernbooks